MW01141730

Equal Play
Stories of
Women Who Dare

Peggy O'Neill

FALCON®

GUILFORD, CONNECTICUT
HELENA, MONTANA

AN IMPRINT OF THE GLOBE PEQUOT PRESS

Falcon is a registered trademark of The Globe Pequot Press.

Cover photos (clockwise from top left): © Corbis; © Carl Skoog, www.carlskoog.com; © Getty Images; Leslie Allen, courtesy Reel Women.

Text and page design: Linda R. Loiewski

Library of Congress Cataloging-in-Publication Data is available.

ISBN 0-7627-1064-0

Manufactured in the United States of America
First Edition/First Printing

For my family.

Contents

Acknowledgments

First of all I'd like to thank my husband, Mike McLeod, for coming home for the last year to an empty refrigerator, a dirty house, and a frazzled wife, without complaining too much. And thanks to that elusive elk that's been keeping him occupied during my mental absence.

Thanks to my parents, Eileen and T. J. O'Neill, for asking me every week when this book would be finished. Thanks also for introducing me to the outdoors, and understanding that the lessons learned outside can sometimes be more valuable than the lessons learned from a lecture.

Thanks to my editor Erin Turner, for her encouragement and for not killing me— or this project—after I offered every possible lame excuse I could think of for an extended deadline. But I really did have a sprained ankle, pneumonia, and the stomach flu all back-to-back at deadline time . . .

But thanks most of all to the women in this book for their inspiration, their time, and the glimpse into their extraordinary lives. Because of them, I am a better outdoorswoman.

Introduction

I don't remember this, but my mother says it happened, so it must be true. Apparently when I was three years old, my oldest brother, Jim, and a family friend named Johnny Osbourne put me on one of those snow-disk sleds, dragged me to the top of a small hill at the Aspen ski area, gave me a push, and sent me careering full speed into the corner of a condo complex. My mother and Johnny's mother watched the whole thing unfold from the window of our condo. Jim and Johnny made a halfhearted attempt to catch up with me before the collision, but they arrived just in time for the impact. Mom and Mrs. Osbourne came running and screaming, thinking that they'd find me with a cracked skull. Instead they found Jim, Johnny, and me rolling around in the snow laughing our heads off. Jim and Johnny were probably just relieved that their mothers would let them live another day. I'm sure I was blissfully unaware of the possible bloody outcome that had miraculously been avoided. I just liked the ride.

That was one of my earliest outdoor experiences, if you don't count the time that my mother went skiing at Crested Butte when she was three months pregnant with me. However it started, my affinity for the outdoors grew with every trip we took from Texas to the Rocky Mountains. That affinity led me to where I am now, an outdoor writer living in Montana. I say *affinity*, because that's what it is. It would be dishonest to call it a passion.

I think if it were a passion, I'd be doing something other than writing about it. I'd be running a business—like Susan Eckert or Lori-Ann Murphy—that caters to women who are curious about adventure. I'd be striving to be the best—like Alison Dunlap or Leslie Ross—at a particular outdoor sport. I'd be dedicated to the outdoor lifestyle—like Amy Bullard—of simplicity and discipline. I'd be encouraging other generations—like Zoe King and Laura Ziemer—to experience the exhilaration of sunlight bouncing off a mountain peak. I'd be fearless—like Mavis Lorenz—to spend time alone deep in the backcountry. I'd be re-creating—like Jody Welch—a scene inspired by nature. Or—like Pam Houston—I'd be teaching readers and writers about identifying the universal truths that can be found during a simple winter camping trip.

This is a collection of their passions. I hope you find them as inspiring as I did. I'm lucky they let me come along for the ride.

Lori-Ann Murphy

Queen of the No-Pride Club

Lori-Ann Murphy, fly-fishing guide and founder of Reel Women. Photo courtesy of Reel Women.

When I arrive at the Reel Women fly shop in Victor, Idaho, there's a sign taped to the door. It reads, ATTENTION FISH PALS—WE HAVE A BABY READY TO POP, SO WE WILL HAVE INCONSISTENT SHOP HOURS. THANKS & FISH ON. There's another sign on the door, too. It says, OPEN, so I walk in. Just then a very pregnant woman peeks out from an office door and says, "Can I help you?" The woman, Reel Women business manager Kim Trafton, was busy teaching her husband how to operate a cash register. Apparently the husband will tackle some of Kim's duties while she recovers from childbirth, which, as the sign indicates, could be at any moment now.

After a few minutes, two other women walk into the shop. Tressa plops into a chair and points out the fact that she went through the bothersome task of applying makeup this morning. Jen worries that the shirt she's picked out for the day may

Just the Facts:
Lori-Ann Murphy

- **Birthplace:** Venice, California.

- **Current home:** Victor, Idaho.

- **Age:** Forty-something.

- **Claim to fame:** Founder of Reel Women fly-fishing guide service and one of the best women fly fishers on the planet.

- **Significant others:** Jezebella (dog); Goldie (former truck); Dottie (current truck).

- **Lori-Ann on self-insight:** "I thought I wanted to be a nurse practitioner. But then I thought I'd kill all my patients 'cause I'd get so fed up with them. 'That wouldn't be good,' I thought."

- **Guiding philosophy:** "Everybody has their own style of casting. I really want people to feel comfortable with their own style."

not be bright enough. This is not common banter for the Reel Women guides, but today is different. Not only is today the first day of the two-day trip down the South Fork of the Snake River that will culminate the fall guide school, but it's also the first day of a two-day video shoot, in which Reel Women will try to show how fun it is to fly fish.

Into the middle of the makeup and wardrobe conversation walks the star of the show, Lori-Ann Murphy, the owner of Reel Women and one of the best female fly fishers in the country. Lori-Ann is dressed in the brightest available REEL WOMEN–emblazoned shirt, which happens to be blazing pink. Her blond hair is the perfect style to accentuate her outdoorsy good looks. And like Tressa and Jen, she has a tasteful scarf tied around her neck that is just the right complement for the ensemble.

Immediately I feel underdressed and undergroomed. But they don't seem to notice. Or at least they don't say so.

■

Lori-Ann Murphy is one of those people whom you can't help but like the moment you meet her. That's because from the moment you meet her she treats you like a friend, something she seems to be in no short supply of.

Lori-Ann is also a name-dropper. Not one of those annoying, pretentious kinds of name-droppers who assume they're cool because they know a few cool people. No, Lori-Ann just has so many damn friends that she can scarcely get through a sentence without mentioning a few hundred of them. She's a charming name-dropper, and she is cool. She's a great storyteller, too. With only the slightest provocation, she'll launch into a story about one of her friends and entertain you until one of two things happens—she notices some rising fish or you interrupt her with a stupid question.

Here's an example. It's a story she told while we drifted down the South Fork, about the time she went fly fishing with Martha Stewart and her entourage in the Wind River Mountains of Wyoming. It's a story, like many of her stories, that she tells without stopping for air.

"That was great. I showed up at five o'clock in the morning in Jackson and she was at the

> **"I'm just drinking my coffee, trying to wake up. And I'm just like, 'Martha Stewart is washing my windshield, she's trying to get the bugs off my windshield.' I couldn't believe it."**

Best Western," Lori-Ann begins, her voice deep, but lively. "She looked like . . . herself. And I said, 'Hi Martha, I'm Lori-Ann.' I had my old truck then, Goldie, which was a 1974, four-by-two Ford. Beautiful old custom truck. I had been guiding every day; I had mosquitoes all over the windshield and everything and, really, it wasn't clean. So we got out to the parking lot and she hops in the truck. And I said, 'You're not going with me.' And she said, 'Yes, I am.' And I said, 'No you're not. You're going in the van and I'm going to follow you down to Pinedale.' And she said, 'Oooh, no.' So she sits in the truck, we pull out of town, and she says, 'Will you pull into this gas station?' And it's now six o'clock in the morning and Martha Stewart is washing my windshield. And I'm just like, 'Martha Stewart . . .'"

Lori-Ann laughs her dry-throated laugh.

"And I'm just drinking my coffee," she continues, "trying to wake up. And I'm just like, 'Martha Stewart is washing my windshield, she's trying to get the bugs off my windshield.' I couldn't believe it."

It might be surprising that this world-renowned fly fisherwoman would know anything about the queen of happy homemaking (this story happened in 1994—pre-ImClone). But Teton Valley living has not left Lori-Ann in the dark when it comes to all-things Martha Stewart.

"It was pretty funny. I had made a wedding cake for my best friend out of Martha Stewart's wedding cake book," Lori-Ann goes on. "And Martha said to me, like on the second day, 'Lori-Ann, I don't think you realize who I am.' And I said, 'Oh, I've a pretty good idea; I made one of your wedding cakes for my best friend.'"

But even with Martha Stewart being, well, Martha Stewart, Lori-Ann Murphy wasn't afraid to be Lori-Ann Murphy.

"We had a fight in the middle of the night." Lori-Ann laughs. "I set up my old North Face tent away from the crew and I had an old brownie wrapper in my jacket. We had all this incredible food packed in on horses; we hiked in 11 miles. Anyway, I went to get my jacket and one of the bears had gone *slash,* grabbed my jacket, mauled my jacket, slobbered all over it. So Martha Stewart was like, 'Well, Lori-Ann, you can sleep with me and Anyetta [Martha's art director].' So here's Martha, here's me, and here's Anyetta. It's one o'clock in the morning . . . I'm exhausted. So I'm just thinking, 'You're next to Martha Stewart, don't snore.' Anyway a bear goes by, stinks to high heaven like twelve Dumpsters, just stinks really bad. And I'm like, 'Well, the bear's just going to the kitchen . . . I'm just gonna try to go to sleep.' This is how exhausted I was. But Martha was sleeping with the whistle in her mouth and so in my left ear, she goes *tweeeeeeeeaaaat*! In which case I go off and I'm just like, 'Jesus Christ,' and just start screaming. And Martha is just like, 'I'm sorry, Lori-Ann, the bear went by and dadadada . . .' And I went, 'You haven't cooked one damn thing on this whole trip and you're supposed to be this incredible cook.'"

"So, what about those scarves you and the rest of the guides wear?" I interrupt.

■

There are other stories, too. There's the time she befriended Leigh Perkins without knowing he was the founder of Orvis; the time she stayed up drinking champagne with fly-fishing matriarch Joan Wulff on the tenth anniversary of Joan's husband's death; and the time she told Kevin Bacon she thought he was a "creepy guy."

But these stories just help explain who Lori-Ann is—a no-nonsense, down-to-earth gal. Or, as she likes to put it, "The queen of the no-pride club."

Lori-Ann Murphy didn't really grow up fly fishing. She just kind of drifted into it, decided she liked it, and went from there. Eventually it became her passion.

"It took me ten years to figure some things out," she tells me as she watches me fumble through a double surgeon's knot. "I didn't know I could tie a small dry fly to 3X, I didn't know your fly line needed to be changed—it'd get cracked and sink. All these little things. I remember sitting down and taking forever to tie a knot. I've just embarrassed myself on so many different occasions."

Eventually the embarrassing moments were outweighed by moments of inspiration and Lori-Ann found herself spending any spare time on the water with a rod.

■

By education, Lori-Ann is a nurse. While living in Seattle and working as an ortho-pedic nurse, she had a sweet schedule of four-day weekends followed by three-day weekends, with a few days of work in between.

"I had it made," Lori-Ann says. "I would just bolt down to the Deschutes on the four-day weekends, and on the three-day weekends I'd head over to the Yakima or out to Hood River. I was gone by that point. And it was so overwhelmingly strong."

On a trip to the Henrys Fork near the Montana–Idaho border, Lori-Ann paid a visit to the Teton Valley. She stopped in the tiny hospital in Driggs just to see what was going on there.

"The doc, Larry Curtis, was there with the housekeeper, and there were fresh cinnamon rolls coming out of the oven," she remembers. "There was this whole full-course noon roast beef meal going on. And I just went, 'Well, this just doesn't hap-pen anywhere on the planet anymore.'"

The hospital offered Lori-Ann a position as a home health-care nurse. She knew she wanted the position, but she decided to take a drive to think things over.

"So I drove up to Grand Targhee and a wolf walks right in front of me," she says. "And I was like, 'That's a wolf.'"

She took the job.

"Right on! Right on! Right on! Go team!" Lori-Ann yells out into the quiet air. One of her guide school students holds up a nice brown trout.

■

While she may not have been a child prodigy fly angler, Lori-Ann was a tomboy in the full sense of the word. She grew up in Venice, California, the oldest of seven kids in a tradi-tional Irish Catholic family.

"I definitely wasn't playing with my Barbies," she says. "My dad used to take me deep-sea fishing off the coast of California. They didn't allow girls on the boat. I was twelve and looked like a boy and my dad would call me Louie."

> **"I definitely wasn't playing with my Barbies. My dad used to take me deep-sea fishing off the coast of California. They didn't allow girls on the boat. I was twelve and looked like a boy and my dad would call me Louie."**

A good student, Lori-Ann cruised through school, which left her plenty of time to be outside. Days were spent on the beach, pitching softball, playing with the population of kids on her block. Whatever she was doing, it was sure to be an adventure.

"And then my girlfriend Janet King, whom I still see—I still see all my girlfriends once a year. They all married the guy they went to the prom with and have three kids. I'm the only one who left Venice. Anyway, Janet's parents would take us skiing and backpacking. I always gravitated toward fun. And my mom used to say, 'Lori-Ann, all you care about is your goddamn fun.' Which is true. And I guess if you're going to be cursed by anything, you might as well be cursed by that."

> **"I always gravitated toward fun. And my mom used to say, 'Lori-Ann, all you care about is your goddamn fun.' Which is true. And I guess if you're going to be cursed by anything, you might as well be cursed by that."**

Nursing school was an obvious choice for Lori-Ann. Her mother and her aunt Ruth, who set up army hospitals during World War II, were both nurses.

"I thought I wanted to be a nurse practitioner," Lori-Ann says. "But then I thought I'd kill all my patients 'cause I'd get so fed up with them. 'That wouldn't be good,' I thought."

Lori-Ann continued nursing even after she started Reel Women in 1993. But fishing eventually won out. "I'm glad I have that skill [nursing], but I'm glad I'm not still in it," she says. "Health care is so frustrating to me now. You know, I actually see my profession changing. I see staying in fishing but I don't know what direction it will take. And I think that I can't believe I'm forty-five and someday I might be older."

Lori-Ann stops rowing to point out an eagle and then immediately looks back to the water.

"Oop, oh yeah. I'm going to pull over here. You can either leave on that little Prince or change to a dry," she tells me.

■

What Lori-Ann had in mind with Reel Women was something unique—an opportunity for women to learn how to fly fish in the company of other women, and an opportunity for women who already fish to go on women-only trips.

"At the beginning, we were inspired by women," Lori-Ann says. "We had the women's school and the women wanted to go on women-only trips. And I was like, 'Okay, let's just have fun and go on these fun trips.' But then I realized that if we wanted to make this a business, if we wanted to survive, then we were going to have to learn about business, which was a huge learning curve for me."

Today, in addition to the women-only trips and schools, Reel Women leads coed trips and offers a coed professional guide school—and male guides are part of the team. Fifty percent of the students in this week's guide school are male. What's the difference?

"When people ask me that, I think the common thing we hear the most is that women are better listeners so maybe they'll be better anglers, better guides," Lori-Ann says. "But I can't really make any gender-specific comments about that. It depends on the learner and the personality. I've certainly seen just as many women who are as wound up as men. At first I thought what we did for women in the guide school was tremendous. In terms of confidence, you'd see these huge shifts, and people would make life changes. But since we've been doing the coed guide school, you see the guys do the same thing."

One of Lori-Ann's male graduates gave up forty-eight Avis rental car agencies for a career in fly fishing.

"Why don't you try this white streamer," Lori-Ann says as she pulls over river right. "There's some fish in there."

■

After stripping the Playboy Bunny all afternoon with no success, I have to rethink my strategy. It's becoming apparent that the fish in the South Fork of the Snake won't turn their heads for just any old fly, no matter how attractive.

"Why don't you try a Copper John?" Lori-Ann offers. She stops rowing long enough to dig the nymph pattern out of her fly box and hands it to me to tie on.

I try again.

"You have a nice cast," Murphy says.

Two minutes later, maybe because no one in the five years I've been fly fishing has ever said that to me and the one-and-only compliment made me self-conscious, I backcast my rig into a tree.

After cursing like a sailor and blowing my newly achieved reputation as a good caster, I realize that that first fly-fishing compliment accompanied another first—my first time fishing with another woman. Why hadn't I done this before? Wait a minute, is she just trying to be nice?

"It's more of an outfitting philosophy," Lori-Ann says. "Everybody has their own style of casting. For me, I really want people to feel comfortable with their own style. You can say, 'Why don't you try this,' or 'Why don't you try that,' and it might help them discover something about their own style. It's about getting people to be comfortable with their cast. If you go out and point out everything they're doing wrong, then they're not going to want to fish again."

So my cast isn't that great after all? I don't ask this out loud; I'm not sure I really want to know the answer.

Instead I ask, "So who's the most famous person you've ever fished with?"

■

If you've seen the movie *The River Wild*, you may or may not remember Meryl Streep fly fishing. Before the movie became the "creepy guy" vehicle for Kevin Bacon, it contained a little more fly-fishing footage, and Lori-Ann helped orchestrate the scenes.

"That was the best job I ever had," she states matter-of-factly. "I was still doing the home health stuff and I came home one day and there was a message on the machine that said, 'Lori-Ann, this is Universal Studios and we were wondering if you'd be interested in teaching Meryl Streep and Kevin Bacon how to fly fish for our upcoming movie *The River Wild*. I was like, 'Oh my God, Jezebella'—that's my dog. I immediately typed up a résumé and sent it off. But it definitely was 'a moment.' I couldn't believe I was hearing that."

Lori-Ann spent four months on the set in Montana with the cast and crew.

"Meryl Streep is incredible," she says, launching into another story. "She's an incredible mimic. And one time on dailies she—from being around me—she makes this comment and then goes, 'Geez Louise.' And I just go, 'Oh my God, that was me.' She was mimicking me. Because that's not her. She's East Coast and that's not something she'd say. She was forty-three at the time, and she did that film for her children. She wanted them to see that she could be in an adventurous role at that age. That was her intent. By the end of it, I was like, 'What do you think?' And she said, 'You know, I'd rather be sitting in the Boston Tea Room.'"

Another Reel Women guide fly fishing on the South Fork of the Snake River in Idaho. Photo by Peggy O'Neill.

"Ooh, there's some fish. See their heads coming up?"

■

The second and last day of the trip down the South Fork, Lori-Ann spends with the camera crew. The September morning sun provides perfect backlighting through the orange, red, and yellow foliage on the banks of the river. She has the day to tell the camera why fly fishing is fun. But I imagine she'll explain it the way she explained it to me.

"It literally brings you right to the present," she told me yesterday as we waited for rising fish. "Suddenly, you're looking at this fly, a swallow will come down and eat this fly, and then a fish head comes up. I'm not thinking of any of my personal crises or work. I became addicted to that feeling.

"I liked it so much that I traded in my 1968 Mercury Comet—two-door, blue Naugahyde—for my truck and then a bigger truck and then you start thinking about trucks. And my big truck is named Dottie for 'damn outrageous truck'—total macho rigs. But they're fun and they drive fast.

"It's good medicine. Even now, I'm going through a changing, shifting time in my life and I have a tendency to get inside my own head and I just don't want to spin out there and I just want to be here in my heart. I'll head down to the Teton River and I'll feel so much better. I feel so lucky to have that. And I feel that's sort of my purpose."

A moth flutters to the water and drifts toward the bank.

"Here it comes," Lori-Ann says. A big rainbow rolls across the surface and disappears. The moth is gone.

Susan Eckert

Adventure Inspiration

**Susan Eckert, posing with a
Samburu dancer in Kenya.**
Photo copyright
AdventureWomen, Inc.

Susan Eckert has a bison head hanging on the wall in her living room. Bison heads are not an unusual ornament for living room walls in Montana. But somehow, among the West African masks, the Tibetan rugs, the Peruvian bowls, and the Arizona sand paintings, the head seems a little out of its element in this particular living room, which overlooks the Bridger Mountains just north of Bozeman.

"He's beautiful, isn't he?" Susan says when she catches me looking at him. "When I moved here, the idea of having an animal on my wall was totally repulsive. But you change. You get to appreciate things and look at things in a different way. So many people look at hunters like, 'Oh, you shouldn't hunt.' Hey, it's not my place to tell people they shouldn't hunt. I'm not gonna hunt. But it's a way of life in Montana. You can't come from another state and tell people how to live here."

Just the Facts:
Susan Eckert

- **Birthplace:** Chicago area.

- **Current home:** Bozeman, Montana.

- **Age:** Fifty-something.

- **Claim to fame:** Founder of AdventureWomen travel service, which offers hiking, canoeing, horseback riding, and cross-country skiing trips in the United States and all over the world.

- **Number of continents visited:** Seven.

- **Number of males with whom she shares her home:** One (a stuffed bison head).

- **Formative experience:** Three years as a Peace Corps public health worker in West Africa. "How wonderful it is to be in another part of the world and live in another culture!"

- **Guiding philosophy:** "Women travel differently from men. . . . For men, it's not the journey that's important but the destination."

That's a good philosophy to have if you're an adventure traveler. And it's a philosophy she shares with the women who accompany her on the twenty-five or so trips she sets up each year through her business, AdventureWomen.

■

The year 2002 marked the twentieth anniversary of AdventureWomen, an adventure-travel company that caters to women over thirty years of age.

"Twenty years ago, adventure travel was not the thing to do," Susan says.

And it wasn't supposed to be the thing that Susan did, either. Until the age of thirty-five, Susan had planned a career in public health. She took the necessary steps—she went to a small liberal arts college and graduated with a degree in biology. She joined the Peace Corps and was assigned a tour in West Africa, where she worked for three years in public health. She returned to the United States, married, and began pursuing a PhD in public health while living in the Chicago area.

"I never finished the PhD," Susan says. "I thought to myself, 'I can't do this for the rest of my life. I can't work in an office for the rest of my life. I have to do something outside.' I wanted to take people to see other cultures. I wanted to travel."

It was a big decision. And in hindsight it was a wise one. But it was also a decision that precluded other choices.

"I never made the decision not to have kids," she says. "It just happened. I couldn't have done this if I had a family. I did not make a conscious decision not to have a family. I'm really glad I did what I did. I am really happy with the way my life has turned out. But then again, if I would have had a family, I would have said, 'I'm really happy with the way my life turned out.'"

As it turned out, Susan divorced her husband after ten years of marriage. Her clients have, in a way, become the surrogate children to whom she can show the world.

■

Her client base started out small, as did her annual itinerary. But she did the best with what she had to work with, including her $25,000 life savings.

Still living in Chicago, Susan took advantage of the weekend warriors who wanted a reprieve from the city. Her first trip was a cross-country ski weekend to Wisconsin.

> **"Before I moved to Montana, Africa was really my spiritual home. I had to go back there every year."**

"I started the business doing weekend trips," Susan says. "The weekend trips were a good springboard for women to see if they wanted to go on longer trips. Then I expanded slowly."

From cross-country skiing, AdventureWomen trips expanded to include horseback riding, canoeing, and hiking. "The first trips were down and dirty," Susan says. "They were the kind of trips you'd think of now as extreme. We carried our canoes and backpacks."

In addition to the weekend trips, Susan couldn't help but share Africa with clients willing to sign up: "Before I moved to Montana, Africa was really my spiritual home. I had to go back there every year." Despite having "zippo money," Susan's business blossomed and her dream to travel was coming true.

"I was so focused. I wasn't nervous; I was just so determined. I probably lost less sleep then than I do now." Like others in the travel industry, Susan has felt the impact of September 11. "I had no money. You know, I had nothing to lose. When you don't have a house and animals and responsibilities and you're paying other people, it's kind of nice not to have those responsibilities. You can do a lot with your life when you don't own things."

Now in her midfifties, Susan has a house filled with souvenirs from places around the world. She calls it her dream house. She also has a horse, a cat, and a

Tibetan terrier named Saki. In addition, the home serves as the office for AdventureWomen, which, besides Susan, employs a full-time office manager and another part-time helper. Except for the bison head, all the residents and employees at the house are female.

Susan and Cherie Newman, the office manager and Web master, have nothing against men. They call on them when something like plumbing problems, furniture moving, or coffee machine repairs come up. But when it comes to traveling, Susan and Cherie find that women make the best companions.

"You can do a lot with your life when you don't own things."

"When it's just women, they can relax and just be themselves," Cherie says. "I like the way it changes women, how their whole perspective can change. It's something so completely outside our everyday lives."

"Women travel differently than men," Susan observes. And she's traveled enough to know. "There are probably only a few women who haven't had a hike ruined by the competitive nature of a male companion. For men, it's not the journey that's important but the destination."

■

On a particularly hot July afternoon, thirteen women from around the country gather in a parking lot in Yellowstone National Park. They are about to take a hike together. For some, this will be the first time they've set foot on a trail that wasn't paved or wasn't deep in the heart of a big city. For others, it's the opportunity to add another entry to their hiking résumé. But for all, it's an adventure of a lifetime.

Ranging in age from forty-three to sixty-four, these hikers are on a weeklong trip with Susan's AdventureWomen. Their itinerary includes four day-hikes in Yellowstone National Park and a day of rafting on the Yellowstone River. Susan does not accompany the women this time. After hosting the adventurers at a barbecue at her home, she entrusts them to guide and naturalist Barbara Batey. Susan remains in Bozeman to make the painstaking plans for next year's AdventureWomen itineraries.

Half of the women on this trip are married, the other half happily single or divorced. Either way, these women have chosen to forgo the company of men to travel in the comfort of an all-female party. Even though the women arrived as

Susan Eckert in her Bozeman, Montana, home, decorated with the trappings of her round-the-world adventures. Photo by Peggy O'Neill

strangers to each other, after only a day together they act like best friends. They are mothers, bank executives, nurses, paralegals, teachers, pilots, computer techies—females ready to be challenged.

One by one they step out of the AdventureWomen van, take a final visit to the last real toilet they'll encounter for 9 miles, slather on sunscreen and bug dope, and take a swig of water from their Nalgene bottles before storing them in their well-stocked day packs.

The mothers among them make sure their companions have enough water and an adequate SPF sunscreen.

Dressed in colorful CoolMax T-shirts and bandannas, the hikers file in behind their guide Barbara, who, at more than 6 feet tall, towers over her charges like a mother hen with curious chicks. Conversation among the bunch ranges from how this hike compares to others they've done to a discussion on what makes some folks tastier to pesky mosquitoes. No talk of husbands, kids, or responsibilities is heard.

"We want to discuss other things," says a sixty-something-year-old adventurer from Arkansas whose day pack is decorated with patches from other hikes in other places with other groups. "We want to talk about the things we are seeing around us."

The women proceed slowly, taking time to see everything there is to see. July in Yellowstone is crazy if you stay on the roads and only bother to walk a few feet from your car. But the trails are less traveled and the rewards are infinite. Wildflowers brush the women's hiking boots as they amble by, bighorn sheep graze unfazed by the gawking hikers, and bison stand noble as they are preserved eternally on film.

None of the details are lost on the women. Even a patch of dandelions and a faraway plume of smoke, both unwanted summer guests to residents of the Rocky Mountains, draw a certain appreciation from the women. What's new and what's different from their normal routine is beautiful—or at least something worth noting.

A strange ball of hair lies in the middle of the trail. Several women trample it before it comes to the attention of a curious hiker from Connecticut. It looks suspiciously like a regurgitated hairball from a cat.

"What is this?" someone asks. The rest of the women stop in their tracks and gather around for Barbara's explanation.

Barbara says it's an owl pellet—a ball of fur, bones, and teeth that are the indigestible parts of an owl's diet. Sometimes an owl swallows its prey whole, she says, and the indigestible parts are compacted in the owl's stomach, then regurgitated.

The subject is again discussed over lunch halfway through the hike, above the silty blue Yellowstone River. Other lunchtime topics include the differences between a grizzly track and a black bear track, the fact there are indeed folks out there who make a hobby of studying scat, the realization that at this moment they are probably being watched by several species of wildlife, and the persistent and undeniable call of nature. The idea of peeing in the woods is something new to several of the women.

"I haven't done that since I was eighteen years old and drunk," laughs an Ohio hiker.

As the day heats up and the miles stretch on, one hiker falls behind. The temperature at such an altitude takes its toll. The women adjust their pace to accommodate everyone and stop at the nearest shady spot. Again, the mothers in the group make sure everyone else has enough water, trail mix is shared, and when all are sufficiently rested and refueled, the group travels the last 2 miles to the parking lot together.

Such a large group of women draws attention and questions, which the hikers gladly field. Most of the questions come from other women who are traveling with their husbands and families, who seem eager to find out how to become part of such a group. Why they prefer to travel in the company of other women is a question they think has an obvious answer.

"It's more stimulating," says the Arkansas woman.

"It's more relaxing," says a hiker from Florida.

"Men go too fast to appreciate what they're passing up," says another from Texas. "For women the journey is the destination."

∎

Susan credits the Peace Corps with changing her perspective on life. If you ask her what the best thing she's ever done is, she doesn't stop to think about it. Even with seven continents' worth of traveling experiences, Susan says unequivocally that the Peace Corps was the best.

"It's a good thing to have my own business and it's a wonderful life," she says. "But the thing that has shaped everything that I've done since the Peace Corps is the Peace Corps experience. You gain a whole new perspective of what it is to be, number one, an American, and number two, just a human being. We [Americans] are a minority, and the rest of the world doesn't live like we live. It opens your eyes to what opportunity we have here. And how wonderful it is to be in another part of the world and live in another culture."

"Lots of lives change by just making a decision to do something different."

It might be a particularly female perspective, but that's probably why her business is successful. By understanding the female perspective, she can give her clients what they want and make them comfortable even when they're on the other side of the planet.

"So many women have never done anything on their own before, or never made a decision that they needed something different in their lives. And then they come on a trip and it's such an eye-opening experience. Their self-confidence increases so much, and they can act and make decisions that they wouldn't have without this experience. Lots of lives change by just making a decision to do something different."

■

The bison head is nameless. He hangs impressively on the wall opposite Susan's fireplace, gazing down in an eternal gesture of wisdom. His strength has been reduced to that of any other wall hanging. But still, in Susan's house he is beautiful. Along with the African baskets, the Moroccan rugs, the Italian bowls, and the iron sculptures from Timbuktu, he is a reminder of the way travel breeds compassion and the importance of having an adaptable perspective.

Alison Dunlap

Some Girls Have All the Luck

Mountain bike World
Cup champion Alison Dunlap
keeps a collection of bikes in
her home in Colorado Springs.
Photo by Peggy O'Neill

It would be easy to hate Alison Dunlap. She's just so darn perfect. She's smart, she's fit, she's pretty, she's organized, and she's the best female mountain biker in the world.

Just look at her résumé: It lists things like world elite mountain bike champion, five-time cyclo-cross champion, and two-time Olympian (road cycling in 1996, mountain biking in 2000). The newest addition to her long list of accomplishments is mountain bike World Cup champion, a title she claimed in September 2002.

Another reason to yank on her perky ponytail is the fact that if she hadn't chosen to become a professional cyclist, she had a backup plan. Instead of being Alison Dunlap, world's best female mountain biker, she could have accepted an offer to join a PhD program at the University of Utah to become Dr. Alison Dunlap, desert ecologist.

Just the Facts:
Alison Dunlap

- **Birthplace:** Denver, Colorado.
- **Current home:** Colorado Springs, Colorado.
- **Age:** Thirty-something.
- **Claim to fame:** Best female mountain bike racer in the world.
- **Says who?:** Says the world elite mountain bike championships, the cyclo-cross championships (five wins), the Olympics (two-time participant), and the mountain bike World Cup championships.
- **Guiding philosophy:** "Dreams really do come true."

It's enough to make you want to scream, "Why can't you just make a mistake once in a while, so the rest of us don't feel so bad about ourselves!"

But then you meet her and you can't help but like her. She's just so darn nice.

If Alison Dunlap weren't so nice, she could have easily kicked my ass and left me eating her dust on that sunny November morning in Colorado Springs. But one look at my decrepit mountain bike, my holey shorts, and my skinny legs, and she must have taken pity on me and decided it would be "an easy day" for her training schedule.

We took the wide, gravelly Pikes Peak Greenway, which cuts through downtown Colorado Springs and winds about 20 miles to the U.S. Air Force Academy. Even for my pathetic mountain biking skills, the trail was not a technical challenge. It was the pace that Alison maintained that threw my lungs into convulsions. Sensing my struggle to keep up, she slowed to a pace where I could spit out a couple of questions between gasps of air, and she answered in long, articulate narratives. I can't tell you what she said, however, because it took my complete concentration to keep pedaling.

We rode together for about two hours. I wish I could say it was a gnarly ride and that we both came back covered in mud and blood. But I made the only extreme maneuver, when I failed to unclip from my pedal in a timely fashion and fell like a log onto the dirt. I don't think Alison saw me, or maybe it was the niceness kicking in again and she didn't say anything about it.

The odd thing about biking with Alison is how inconspicuous she is. Riding past other mountain bikers, I would try to gauge their level of recognition of the most fantastic female mountain biker on the planet. Plus, I wanted them to see how cool I was for being her companion for a day. Except for other bikers whom she knew by name, though—about half of those we encountered—no one gave us a second look. Alison is not flashy or pretentious, and beneath a bike helmet and sunglasses she could be just another weekend warrior for all anybody else knew. She could be.

■

Two hours later, breathless and a little bruised, I sit with her in the backyard of her cute but modest house, in a cute but modest neighborhood in downtown Colorado Springs. A Subaru sits in the driveway, and a muffin pan lies in the yard. A curious squirrel steals the last crumbs from the ill-fated pastries, which were the well-meaning but overbaked project of her husband, Greg Frozley, also a mountain bike racer.

"He's a good cook but he doesn't do it very often," she says. "I don't think he likes to follow a recipe. He made those muffins and went downstairs to work on his bike and he didn't hear the buzzer go off. So they burned and he was so upset. He was like, 'I wanted to do something really nice for you and show you that I could make these muffins and I burned the hell out of them.'"

This is what life at home is like for a world-class athlete—well, at least for Alison Dunlap—ordinary, calm, and did I say modest?

It's the way she likes it. And it must be the opposite of the competitive frenzy on the cross-country course or the cyclo-cross course, events Dunlap excels in. Look through almost any cycling magazine, and there are photos of her dropping through rock gardens, photos of her slogging through mud, photos of her competing with a cast on her wrist, and photos of her basking in the glory of victory.

Dunlap says she keeps copies of all-things Alison (not in plain view, however)— stories, photos, medals, race mementos—not so much as badges of honor, but more as a reminder that "dreams really do come true," a phrase she signs along with her autograph.

Ask her what it's like to be the best in the world at something and her eyes light up as if the compliment is something new.

"It's really amazing," Dunlap gushes. "I still can't believe that I won the world championship. It was such a huge goal of mine. You almost don't ever think it could happen to you—that's just too good, something too wonderful. And it finally did. And it was such an incredible thing. On the one hand it was like, 'You know, I deserve it.' I've trained for fourteen years. I've raced and I'm clean and I'm a nice person. I deserve to be the best in the world. But still, with everything that goes on in cycling, especially drug use, it's very hard to say to yourself, 'If I train hard and work really hard then I will win.' It doesn't necessarily happen."

■

Indeed, Dunlap's life has been a series of stories that begin with hard work and end with success.

"I know as a kid and a teenager, it was really important to me to not really be the best of all my friends at something, but to always do the absolute best job I could possibly do. I wouldn't say that I was a perfectionist but I had these really high standards. Even as a kid I always wanted to get straight As. I knew that I could and if I didn't, I was letting myself down. Not anybody else. But I was letting myself down."

Of course she graduated from high school at the top of her class and went to a good college, where she did well enough to get that doctoral program offer. But somewhere in there, that predictable equation of hard work equals success didn't add up—she failed to make the college soccer team.

"It was devastating," she says. "I remember being a little panicked. I was a freshman and all I heard about was the freshman fifteen—how freshmen typically gain fifteen pounds their first year. I was horrified at the thought. So I said, 'I gotta find another sport to do.' Then I saw a sign for the cycling club."

> **"As a kid and a teenager, it was really important to me . . . to always do the absolute best job I could possibly do."**

In a rare case of arrogance, Dunlap entered the world of cycling like the proverbial bull charging into a china shop. The only preparation she had was a high-quality road bike she had purchased with high school graduation gift money from her grandparents. She made her choice not so much because she wanted a good bike, but rather just because she thought it looked cool.

"There was this century ride down in Florence [a town near Colorado Springs, where she attended Colorado College]," she recalls. "I'd never done anything like that, so I was like, 'I'm going to go do a century ride.' I couldn't get anyone to do it with me, and I look back at it now and I'm like, 'Well, obviously not, it's 100 miles.' So I went down there all by myself, and I had my nice, cool bike and I carried a backpack on my shoulders and had these goofy riding shoes that must have been fifty years old. But I was bound and determined to do this century ride. I finished but it took me over nine hours. And then I couldn't sit down for the next couple of days because my butt was so sore."

True to the Dunlap spirit, though, Alison was inspired rather than humiliated by that first century ride. She extended her membership in the college cycling club even though she was the only female. It could have had something to do with the doughnuts, however.

> **"I was bound and determined to do this century ride. I finished but it took me over nine hours. And then I couldn't sit down for the next couple of days."**

"I remember the first time we rode to Woodland Park [outside of Colorado Springs], and the other riders said, 'We're going to the Donut Mill.' And I was like, 'What's the Donut Mill?' I thought that was the greatest thing in the world—we're going to eat doughnuts on our ride. And also I remember the first race I went to—it was not collegiate, it was actually USCF [United States Cycling Federation] up in Denver. My race was at 7:30 in the morning, so for breakfast we went to Dunkin' Donuts. So the reason I loved cycling was because it was more social."

And those doughnuts never went to her hips; they actually fueled her on to a promising career. By the end of her senior year in college, she got licensed with USA Cycling and won her first race at the beginner level. "Oh, that was the greatest day," she said. "I was just so thrilled. I got my first taste of victory, and I was like, 'This just makes it all worth it.' That was when I really knew I was hooked on racing."

Alison continued to excel in cycling and actually competed in the 1996 Olympics for the U.S. road cycling team. But a head injury from a cycling accident the year before caused her to take time off and check out a different scene. By that time she had met her would-be husband Greg, who was competing in mountain bike races.

"What I did was I followed Greg around to all his mountain bike races," Alison says. "That was my first exposure to mountain bike racing, and I thought it was just the coolest thing in the world. You know, outside in the cool ski areas and everybody's really friendly. I was just like, 'This is great!' That started me thinking."

Fed up with the politics of the road bike scene, especially after the '96 Olympics, Alison switched sports. She had done a little mountain biking for fun in college and with Greg.

"So I put the word out that I was looking for a team and GT Bicycles called me up out of the blue and said, 'We'd love to hire you.' And so I got a contract within two days and all of a sudden I was a mountain biker. But I knew I was a good rider. And again, I knew I would probably do well if I trained hard, and had all this great fitness from the road (cycling)." She was good enough, in fact, to place seventh at the 2000 Olympics in mountain biking.

Alison says that there's a big difference between road cycling and mountain biking. The latter fits in better with her personality. The rewards of training hard are more apparent and personal.

> **"I like the fact that mountain biking is an individual sport. There's no one out there who can help you. You're on your own. And if you do well, it's 100 percent you. . . . If you don't do well, it's your own fault."**

"I like the fact that mountain biking is an individual sport," she says. "There's no one out there who can help you. You're on your own. And if you do well, it's 100 percent you. Whereas on the road, if you're a sprinter and you sit in the entire race and you win the race, you get all the glory but you didn't do anything—your teammates did it all for you. I miss the team tactics of road racing, but I like the fact that in mountain biking it's you. If you don't do well, it's your own fault."

That's why Alison takes her training so seriously. She trains hard all year, with the exception of October, which she sets aside for fun and relaxation with Greg. Her training week is a combination of technical rides, cardio rides, and strength training rides. It's all on the bike and it's all outside.

"Competitive mountain biking is still really fun for me," she says. "If it wasn't, I would quit. It's so hard that it's got to be fun or it's not worth it. It definitely is a job. I look at it as a job, and I think that has helped me in a lot of ways because it's really raised my professionalism in the way I approach the sport. Say it's cold and yucky outside, but it's your job, you get paid to do this, you need to go out and ride your bike. So I do, and I don't complain. I just have to do it. I have to go to work today."

Not a bad career path that was inspired from fear of the freshman fifteen. At 5 feet 6 inches, the 125-pound Alison can take as many trips as she wants to the Donut Mill. "With cycling you can pretty much eat whatever you want to eat," she says.

I knew there was something about her I didn't like.

Lena Conlan

Having Her Own Way

**Lena Conlan in her
favorite fuzzy red vest.**
Photo by Peggy O'Neill.

The breakfast ingredients at the Conlan house are nothing out of the ordinary: cereal, toast, milk, coffee, orange juice. But professional kayaking guide and lifelong camper Lena likes orange juice with her Post Banana Nut Crunch—or, more precisely, orange juice *in* her Banana Nut Crunch. She knows you might think that's weird, so she explains it.

"I don't want you to think I'm really tired or something and don't know what I'm doing. I like it this way," she says in a Swedish accent that's thicker than you might expect from someone who's lived in the United States for half of her forty years.

The juice habit is something she picked up somewhere in the world where the milk is unpredictable, she says. And given the itinerary of Lena's life, that could be

Just the Facts:
Lena Conlan

- **Birthplace:** Sweden.

- **Current home:** Bozeman, Montana.

- **Age:** Forty-something.

- **Claim to fame:** Co-owner of Crossing Latitudes, a travel business specializing in guided kayaking, hiking, and skiing trips in Scandinavia.

- **Age the first time she wore a dress:** Fifteen.

- **Careers she gave up to pursue a lifetime outdoors:** The ministry; teaching school; professional table tennis.

- **Guiding philosophy:** "Good EB" or good expedition behavior—being kind to other campers so they will be kind in return.

almost anywhere. As a full-time instructor for the National Outdoor Leadership School (NOLS) for more than ten years, Lena ate that same cereal-and-orange-juice breakfast in Mexico, Patagonia, Chile, and countless other places. And as a co-owner with her husband, Tim, of Crossing Latitudes, a travel business that specializes in kayaking and hiking trips in Scandinavia, she's gone milkless on almost every coast of Norway and Sweden.

Besides her breakfast choice, Lena has other quirks. They are things that might not be considered quirks for other people, but for someone like Lena, they seem contrary to her character. For instance, she likes ABBA. True, it would probably be considered unpatriotic for a Swede not to like one of the most famous Swedish exports. But Lena likes to crank ABBA when she's vacuuming. The music adds to the feverish frenzy with which she tackles housework, something that in itself is hard to imagine Lena doing. But housework is something that needs to be done. And for Lena, anything worth doing is not only worth doing well, it's worth doing your best.

"I want to do things the quickest and most efficient way without losing quality," she says. "So I compete with myself to see how well and how fast I can do things. I have very high expectations for myself but not for other people. It drives some people crazy. For me, vacuuming is like a workout. I always try to better my time. From the smallest thing to the largest thing, I push it."

It's like there's a theme song running through her mind at all times: "Anything *I* can do, I can do better." It's a theme that probably started when she was a child, the middle sister of three and the daughter of the director of the largest YMCA camp in Sweden.

"Basically, every weekend we would go to camp," Lena says. "And as soon as school was out in early June, we would go to camp. It was an all-boys camp until I turned ten years old and Dad said one day, 'Lena I've got a great surprise for you. Come on into my office.'"

Lena's reaction to the camp going coed was less than tolerant. She and her sisters had been constant queens of the camp, after all.

"So I said, 'Girls! Dad, they're totally lame. I see them at school and they can't play soccer or sail or canoe.' I couldn't believe he would do this to me. But sure enough, the next summer there was a girls' session and it turned out to be

> **"I said, 'Girls! They're totally lame. . . . They can't play soccer or sail or canoe.' "**

great. Now I wasn't just the camp director's daughter who tried to tag along with all the guys. Now I could be a camper for real and stay in a cabin for the two-week sessions. And of course, I always knew all the games and activities and traditions so it was pretty easy for me to be a good camper. My cabin tended to win everything because I already knew the rules."

■

One of the things that you notice when you talk to Lena is that she's childlike. Not in a bad way; it's more like you can imagine exactly what she was like as a child because she oozes the same energy, animation, and pure exuberance as a child on the first day of summer vacation. It's because of these qualities that you can see the lithe, blond forty-year-old transform into the lithe, blond twelve-year-old while she's telling you a story from the couch in her Bozeman living room. She becomes the girl from your childhood whom you were always a little intimidated by because of her natural athleticism, natural beauty, natural intelligence, and natural confidence. She's that annoying girl who raised her hand every time the teacher asked a question. You didn't want to like her, but you couldn't help it because she was just so much fun to be around.

"We had two foster sisters when I was growing up," Lena says out of the blue. "These girls were from an alcoholic's home and were being beaten, and they were the ones everyone at school picked on. One of them had red hair. That was reason enough to tease her. When I found out they were going to live with us, I was like, 'Okay, she can live in my house, but I'm not going to talk to her.' The first day I didn't say a word. The next day, I was like, 'You can bike to school with me, but

One of the four-footed participants in a Lena Conlan adventure. Photo courtesy of Lena Conlan, Crossing Latitudes.

don't talk to me.' By the fourth day, we were best friends."

Lena pauses a minute, then continues, "We have all these mean thoughts about people, basically because we are scared or we don't know them. And if you give someone a chance, most likely they are going to be really good people."

■

The Conlans' kitchen is equipped with pink appliances, complemented by patterned, floral wallpaper. Not by choice, I'm sure. But Lena's accepted the 1950s decor with the grace of a polite house guest. Really, even though she and Tim have owned the house for more than ten years, she probably feels more at home in a tent pitched somewhere along the shores of Scandinavia. To understand Lena's taste in home decoration, you might do better to head to the basement where she keeps the sleeping bags.

Lena's summer-camp lifestyle continued uninterrupted until she was sixteen. "And then something traumatic happened," Lena says. "Dad passed away. He had sinus cancer." Lena says it felt weird to return to the YMCA camp where her father had worked, so she applied to work at camps in Switzerland and Germany.

"I took the train down to Switzerland," she says. "I remember thinking, '"Oh, my God. I'm going to die. I can't do this. I'm not cut out for this. Why did I apply for this job?'"

It wasn't the best summer of her life. Campers didn't take her seriously or trust in her capabilities. "When I got home, I told Mom, 'I can't believe you let me do that.

Never let your sixteen-year-old daughter go off on her own like that.' And she was like, 'Well, what would you have done if I'd said, No, you can't go.' Of course, I would have been upset and I would have gone."

With the same sense of hotheaded independence and adventure, Lena decided that her family should move to a new town. She did all the research and then one day announced to her mother that they should all move to northern Sweden to a place called Lycksele. When Lena pronounces it, the rich syllables roll off her tongue like a long, drawn-out poem—*lyck-se-le*.

"I just thought it sounded so cool," she says. "And so I told Mom, 'I think we should move.' And she said, 'Lena, I've been thinking of that, too. Where do you think we should move?' And I said, 'Well, I've already decided. We're moving to Lycksele. There's a job for you there and the schools are good.' My younger sister— oh, she was so pissed! Totally."

But Lena got her way, and the family, minus her college-age sister, moved to Lycksele. "We got there and it was like absolutely mosquito hell. But it only took a couple of weeks and then we loved it."

Lena spent her college years in Lycksele. To fund outdoor expeditions she worked in paper mills during the summers, lifting gigantic rolls of paper.

"All the time I would challenge myself," she says. "I was like, 'Okay. Today, I am only going to carry this tool in my right arm. Next week is left-arm training.'"

■

Between outings with her college outdoor club and her own expeditions, Lena studied. She started her college career majoring in religion, thinking that someday she'd be a minister. To hear her say this is like hearing a three-year-old kid saying he wants to be an accountant. She laughs about it now, but she had a good reason for choosing the ministry.

"I think this was a reaction to the fact Dad died," she says. "And growing up in these camps, we had a service every Sunday. The church service would be outside in the forest or on a cliff by the ocean. It would be much more of what I call now 'good EB'—good expedition behavior. And basically, this was about being kind to the other kids at camp—what you want them to do to you, you have to do to them."

But religious studies just didn't go the way she expected, and by the time Lena had switched her major to elementary school education, thoughts of being a minister were long gone. "As a matter of fact, in June that year, I decided I do not believe in God, I do not believe in Jesus and I don't believe in any greater being either. So I was out."

When she graduated, Lena taught fifth grade, but that desire to spread the word of "good EB" was too strong to spend more than a semester as a schoolteacher. She traveled to the United States, where she climbed at all the hot climbing spots—Yosemite, Eldorado Canyon—and ended up taking an instructor training class with the National Outdoor Leadership School.

> **"Being out for thirty days just climbing and hiking—that was heaven to me."**

"I took the course in the Wind River Mountains [in Wyoming] and loved it," she says. "Being out for thirty days just climbing and hiking—that was heaven to me."

■

At the time Lena met her husband, Tim, she had short blue hair. Lena was selected to fill in for another NOLS instructor on a kayaking course off the Baja Peninsula. She found herself teaching with her future husband. But it wasn't love at first sight.

"The course leader was Tim. He said, 'Isth you haf a hard time understhanding what I'm sthaying, let me know and I'll take out my retainersth.' I'm like, 'What?' So he took something out of his mouth, and repeated what he said. And I'm like, 'Oh, my God. This is going to be a long course, I can't even understand what the guy is saying.' When Tim first met me, he thought I looked like John Denver. I had round glasses, too. He was like, 'Who is this weirdo that looks like John Denver and speaks Swedish?' And I was like, 'Who is this guy with the retainers? I can't even understand what he is saying.' So then after about a week of paddling and camping, I was like, 'I like this guy.'"

Tim and Lena have been together ever since that fateful trip in 1986.

It's a rare occasion when Lena wears a dress. You're more likely to see her in a pair of leather pants—Swedish working pants, she calls them. Apparently, leather working pants are as common in Sweden as Carhartts are in the United States. As Lena recalls, it wasn't until her father's fiftieth birthday that she wore a dress for the first time, and it wasn't by choice.

"I was forced to wear a dress," she says. "So I asked Mom, 'How long do I have to wear this?' And she said, 'You have to wear it until everyone is here.' So I stood in the doorway with a list of everyone we invited, and I said 'Hello' to everyone, and as soon as the last person came, I switched to pants."

Lena likes to wear a particular red furry vest and has an unabashed fondness for romantic comedies, especially the ones where Sandra Bullock plays an oddball-turned-princess. Her work doesn't demand high fashion, makeup, or even a well-groomed appearance. Indeed, going sixty days without a shower or a change of clothes was the norm during her days as a NOLS instructor. But Lena likes to shop.

"I have so many darn clothes here that I just love but never wear. In Sweden, it is so expensive to go out, like out to dinner or for beers. So we grew up understanding that it was a big deal to go out, and you should put some energy into what you are going to wear. So the first ten years of living in the States, I would always change clothes and I would always feel that I was too dressed up. Now I've decided I'm not going to feel that way, I'm going to enjoy my clothes and buy whatever goofy stuff I like."

> **"I was forced to wear a dress. . . . . So I stood in the doorway with a list of everyone we invited, and I said 'Hello' to everyone, and as soon as the last person came, I switched to pants."**

The goofy stuff doesn't include makeup. She says she wears mascara on occasion, but that's it. "I think in college I tried—" She points to her eyelids, "—I can't remember what it is called."

"Eye shadow?" I ask.

"Eye shadow," she says. "But it never really seemed to fit me. And of course I was never into just the basics. I would have blue or something."

■

For her fortieth birthday, Lena asked for a table tennis robot. Don't call it a Ping-Pong robot; Lena won't get mad, but she'll certainly correct your faux pas. The thing sits at one end of the table tennis table and spits balls at her. She loves it.

If she hadn't turned out to be a professional outdoorswoman, she might have turned out to be a professional table tennis player and I would be interviewing the world champ of table tennis. That interview would include the fact that her table tennis career started when she was in third grade and continued through college. Her neighbor, whom she trained with, eventually became a world champion and an Olympic silver medalist.

You could blame her choked table tennis career on her passion for the outdoors. Leading a NOLS lifestyle leaves little room for any material objects, never mind a Ping-Pong—I mean, table tennis—table. But when Tim and Lena bought the house with pink appliances, Lena dug out her old table tennis shoes and paddle— "They call it a racquet in Sweden"—and headed down to the Montana State University table tennis club.

"For me, it was like being born again," she says. "I was like, 'Oh, my God I'm playing table tennis again!' I was totally off at first. As the evening went on, I was beating everyone left and right."

Lena plays with her table tennis cronies every Wednesday and Sunday. Not even a powder day at the local ski area can keep her from the paddle, I mean racquet.

"All my friends think I'm totally weird," she says.

■

The phone rings often at the Conlan house, which doubles as the office for Crossing Latitudes. The phone calls are mostly from folks interested in taking a Scandinavian adventure with Lena and her staff. Everyone who calls gets a catalog, which describes the upcoming year's trips. The latest edition is full of smiling people paddling sea kayaks off the coast of Sweden, hiking rugged peaks in Norway, and backcountry skiing in a place called Jämtland, which is somewhere near the border. There are also a few photos of people trekking with reindeer.

The Crossing Latitudes trips are probably a little tamer than the trips Lena led for NOLS. The "expedition" variety require camping most nights, but a few nights in guest houses and hostels are thrown in for good measure and probably to keep that sense of "good EB" in check. The "inn" trips are just that—days spent hiking, paddling, or skiing are rewarded with a warm, dry bed.

Lena doesn't deny that she can appreciate a real mattress with a real roof over her head. She says if she added up all the nights she's spent camping, it would equal more than five years. But still, she recognizes the value of time spent in a tent.

"Sometimes I wish I was just a NOLS instructor again," she tells me. "And I shouldn't say *just*. That was a simple life and I really got a lot of rewards from being out for a month with a group, getting to know the people really well. Camping for a living. Just experiencing the most spectacular places in the world. And I think of horrendous days with driving rain for three or four days, 40-knot winds, holding on to tents so you won't fly away. Tents snapping, kayaks lifting, just the most extreme conditions. You sit there and you're like, 'I hate this. It sucks. It's so nasty.' And at the same time, you're like, 'Wow, I'm so alive. And I can handle this.'"

But being her own boss brings its own rewards, too. After all, she travels between the two places she calls home. Whether hanging out at her house in Bozeman, vacuuming to ABBA, or paddling along the Salten Coast in Arctic Norway, it's all an adventure.

"My life is where I want my life to be," Lena says.

Zoe King

The Mother of All Ski Bums

Zoe King on Zugspeitze Mountain in Germany.
Photo courtesy of Zoe King.

The sun shines down on Zoe King as she fastens the buckles on her ski boots. She looks up and a middle-age woman approaches her to ask her advice on a problem she's having with her own boots. Apparently the woman has puffy ankles, and her boots cut off the circulation to her feet. She's decided that rear-entry boots might be the ticket; still, the boots don't fit as comfortably as they should. Zoe tells the woman to put lifts under her heels. "It worked for me," Zoe says.

Standing near the top of the chairlift, adjusting her pole straps around her wrists, Zoe attracts another advice seeker. The man slides into a hockey stop next to Zoe and asks her about her skis, which happen to be the same as the ones he's wearing. They're new, and he's unsure whether he likes them. After quizzing Zoe about her experience with them and hearing a favorable report, he skis off, more comfortable with his purchase.

Just the Facts:
Zoe King

- **Birthplace:** Aspen, Colorado.

- **Current home:** Helena, Montana.

- **Age:** Fifty-something.

- **Claim to fame:** Has worked as a fully-certified professional ski instructor around the world.

- **Things she does to fill her spare time:** Bungee jumping, aerobics instructing, cave rafting, sailboarding, paraponting, riding her Harley.

- **Guiding philosophy:** When it comes to skiing, "there's not a perfect answer, there's not a perfect turn. There's a combination. And you have to pull from different things."

If you spend a day skiing with Zoe, make sure you have enough patience to put up with several of these types of encounters. Everyone seems to recognize her as an expert on equipment and technique, especially on her home slopes at the Great Divide Ski Area near Helena, Montana. She'll even offer a few bits of unsolicited advice to you, which could be annoying coming from anybody but Zoe. But Zoe's delivery is subtle, like listening to a friend, or listening to your mother. Humility might be the secret to her success.

"It makes you happy that people want to talk to you," she says. "It's not one-sided. It revitalizes me. It makes me feel good. Not only that I have this knowledge, but that I can help."

Zoe doesn't fit the formula for a ski instructor, which she has done all over the world, or even an aerobics instructor, which she has done for many years. She's a petite fifty-something-year-old who thinks she doesn't ski all that well and has no sense of rhythm.

"I'm not really good at anything," she says. When some people say this, you get the sense that they're fishing for a compliment. But when Zoe says it, you somehow know she means it. She just doesn't let the reality of the statement get in the way of improvement.

"I think there's a difference between striving for excellence and striving for perfection," she says. "I used to think excellence and perfection were the same thing. Now I know better. No matter how good you are at something, there's going to be someone who's better. I found out that striving for excellence is worth all your time and energy."

But no matter how mediocre she thinks she is, she is good enough to be a fully certified professional ski instructor, which qualifies her to teach skiing anywhere in the world she wants to. When she finishes her annual spring-break season in Vail, Colorado, she'll head down to the Professional Ski Instructors of America's National

Academy, where she'll hone her skiing and instructing skills before she takes off to teach some more in New Zealand, whose winter coincides with our summer. She'll fill the gaps between ski instructor gigs with aerobics classes. If it weren't for the fact that she has two grown children and has been married for more than thirty years, you might be inclined to call her a ski bum. Indeed, to call her a ski bum isn't too far off the mark. Maybe a more appropriate title would be "the mother of all ski bums."

> **"I think there's a difference between striving for excellence and striving for perfection. I used to think excellence and perfection were the same thing. Now I know better."**

■

She came late to her ski bumdom, which is odd considering she grew up in Aspen, Colorado. But even fifty years ago, skiing was a sport for the rich. Between school and working at a young age, Zoe didn't have time for it. She skied occasionally, but not nearly as often as you'd like to think an Aspen native could. It really wasn't until after she was married and had two children to help support that the idea of skiing for money occurred to her.

"I was never a competitive skier," she says. "My family thought it was such a waste of time and money. But to me the skiers looked so healthy. They had this

A winter camping workshop with Zoe King. Photo courtesy of Zoe King.

Zoe King speeds downhill. Photo by Eliza Wiley.

spark of life. They were just bouncy and perky and sparkly and fun."

Perhaps it takes a person who is "bouncy and perky and sparkly and fun" to follow the career path that's led to a lifetime of skiing and fitness. Because Zoe wanted to ski and she wanted her kids to ski, she decided that being a ski instructor would be not only fun, but economical as well. The same strategy applied when she took a position at a gym. If she worked at a gym, her kids could go swimming for free.

"I made it my work because I wanted to ski and I wanted the kids to ski. I didn't have to feel guilty about going skiing or going to the gym, because I was going to work."

Needless to say, Zoe's children grew up with a deep appreciation for the outdoors. And Zoe's affinity for teaching and nurturing grew with her children. As I said, taking instruction from Zoe is as easy as listening to advice from your own mother. And that's precisely why it's so easy to be inspired by her.

■

When you reach a certain age—maybe around your midthirties—it's easy to think that life will never be better than it is right at that moment. That your body will only become less fit, your brain less sharp, and your passions less important. It's easy to think that your abilities not only will never improve, but will wane with each passing year.

Zoe proves the opposite. Not only in the way she lives her life, but in the way she teaches.

"I wonder if people think, 'Oh, I can never be really good at that so I'm just not going to bother.' If I thought that, I wouldn't go anywhere. Like I said before, I'm not really good at anything. Any discipline I teach, I can go to a workshop, and I find people way better than me. Most of them younger. Many with an atti-

> **"To me the skiers looked so healthy. They had this spark of life. They were just bouncy and perky and sparkly and fun."**

tude because they are young and they are cute. I could probably find a hundred reasons why I don't belong there. But I don't do that. I walk in and find other women my age and I will be well informed, well read, know what's new in the industry. I'm there to be taught. I'll give it my best shot."

Zoe inspires that attitude in her students, too. In Vail she often teaches women her own age how to ski, which involves conquering certain fears—fear of being injured, fear of losing control, fear of looking ridiculous. But she's passing on something that she's learned through a lifetime of trying new things—it really doesn't matter what other people think. It's ironic, in fact, that someone who is the product of such a self-image machine as Aspen grew up to be so self-confident.

"Maybe as a child, I was just confident with who I was," she says. "We were pretty poor. But people should like you for the way you treat them, for the energy you bring to a relationship. If they don't, they're not worth your time. Gosh, if I let it weigh on my mind, the people that don't like me or the people who think I didn't do something very well, I'd be sad all the time."

If she wanted to beat herself up, she could think about the three times she failed her final ski certification test. She could have given up. But she kept trying . . . and trying. She eventually stopped trying so hard, and that's what worked.

"All of a sudden I realized I had been in search of the perfect turn, the perfect time, the perfect answer to the question. And all of a sudden a light went on. And I said, 'You bozo. The problem is—it *isn't* perfect. There's not a perfect answer, there's not a perfect turn. There's a combination. And you have to pull from different things to lead to an improved skill development. Instead, I would just panic and rack my brain for the one thing that was right. And once I just calmed down and realized, 'Hey, there are just several options here' . . . I passed. And it felt really good. I was in my forties when I finished. I was old. It was intimidating. It was the hardest test I'd ever taken in my whole life."

But you never know what Zoe might try next. Perhaps the hardest test of her life is still to come. She never turns down an opportunity and can claim she's tried, in addition to almost all traditional sports, cave rafting, bungee jumping, sailboarding, and paraponting. One of her other passions is riding her Harley without a helmet—something she's starting to reconsider. There's not much she hasn't tried and if you ask her what adventure might be next on her agenda, she thinks long and hard and can't come up with anything. Then finally she says, "If something new comes along that looks fun, I'll give it a go."

> **"If something new comes along that looks fun, I'll give it a go."**

A few more minutes pass, and she adds, "You know, there is something—ski the Haute Route. I think that would be wonderful. I'll make that my goal. I can meet that goal. It's 100 percent doable."

■

The sunny day continues at the Great Divide. Skiing with someone so confident and perky and popular is indeed inspiring. Lines for the chairlift move fast as Zoe chats happily about what it's like to share a condo with the younger ski instructors at Vail. She admires the young ones who've made skiing their life's work. "I'm energized by hanging out with younger people," she says.

Then she talks about the seventy-something-year-old woman whom she taught to ski several years ago. "She said she had just always wanted to try it and that she had nothing to lose," Zoe says. You can't help but imagine Zoe trying something new twenty years from now, or even teaching something new.

When the chairlift deposits us at the top of Mount Belmont, Zoe asks, "When you reach the top of a run, do you stop and look down at it first, or do you just keep skiing?"

I thought it was just a question asked out of curiosity, but it was one of those subtle tips she's so good at. "When I'm teaching, I try to get my students to feel confident enough in their ability that they don't have to stop and look first," she says.

The rest of the day, I practice taking the plunge.

Leslie Ross

Babe in the Backcountry

Leslie Ross pauses alongside
the Nooksack River after a ski
day in the North Cascades,
Washington.
Photo copyright Carl Skoog,
www.carlskoog.com.

Leslie Ross is small. She hadn't told me that about herself when I spoke with her on the phone. She just said she had long brown hair and would be wearing a red sweater. I had also seen photos of her, so I knew vaguely who to look for when I walked into the Main Street Bistro in Breckenridge, Colorado.

I recognized her instantly. Really, what tipped me off was that she was the only person in the restaurant sitting alone, but the red sweater confirmed it. There was also the unmistakable aura of understated confidence that comes with being a professional athlete, which made me feel a little more relaxed in her presence. It's easy to shrink like a wallflower in the presence of a national champion in the sport to which you aspire. Not that being a national telemark free-skiing champion is anywhere near my grasp, but to be capable enough in a sport to teach others how to do it is an accomplishment worth striving for.

Just the Facts:
Leslie Ross

- **Birthplace:** Vermont.

- **Current home:** Breckenridge, Colorado.

- **Age:** Thirty-something.

- **Claim to fame:** Founder of Babes in the Backcountry, which teaches telemark skiing, backcountry skills, and avalanche safety to women; a national telemark free-skiing champion.

- **Other careers she pursues:** Jewelry designer, motivational speaker, magazine columnist.

- **Guiding philosophy:** "If I say no to this, that's basically like backing down from myself. . . . What is life if I'm just going to hide?"

It was snowing slightly on that November evening in Colorado. Indeed, it was the eve of a storm that ended up dropping enough snow to close part of Interstate 25, but also enough to allow for an early opening of several Colorado ski resorts. If I'd been smart, I would have just stuck around Colorado for another week instead of pushing my little Subaru through white-knuckle conditions on my way home to Montana the next day. After all, I was sitting across a table from not only one of the best female tele-skiers in the nation, but also one of the best tele-teachers. In addition to competing in free-skiing competitions, Leslie runs an organization called Babes in the Backcountry that offers courses for women in telemark skiing, backcountry skills, and avalanche training. But I was already desperately overbudget on money and time, so I knew my brush with tele-greatness would be limited to the few hours with Leslie at the Bistro.

■

When you know your time with someone you admire is limited, you tend to be a little selfish. So when the person in control of the stereo at the Main Street Bistro assumed (and in other circumstances, it might have been a fair assumption) that the entire clientele shared in his affinity for listening to the Beatles' *White Album* at high decibels, I got a little testy.

I wanted to be able to ask Leslie deeper questions than "What did you just say?" "What?" "Can you say that again?" So I asked the waitress, "Do you think you could turn the music down a little?" I think she said she would. A few minutes later, the Beatles were replaced by Cat Stevens at a slightly lower volume. After asking two more times, the music was finally lowered to an almost tolerable level.

I think what I really wanted to know, above all else, was if I would ever be able to ski like Leslie. We are the same age—midthirties; we are about the same size—

she's 5 foot 3, I'm 5 foot 5; we both began as alpine skiers; and we both began our postcollege careers as, well, ski bums. The difference is that she dedicated herself to skiing, whereas I dedicated myself to socializing. And if you're going to live in a ski town, it's best if you are a dedicated skier. That's the only thing that makes working two jobs to make the rent on a two-bedroom condo that you share with four people worth the trouble. I gave up after a couple of seasons. Leslie carved out a career for herself.

It wasn't easy for her, though. Remember, she's small. And ten years ago tele-gear was floppy leather boots and fairly skinny skis; none of it designed for a woman, never mind a small woman.

"The early days for me in trying to get involved in the telemark world were hard," she said. "I couldn't find equipment. All the clothes were too big. I remember my first couple of years, I refused to buy another pair of ski pants because they would have been men's pants. I just ended up putting more duct tape on my pants from college."

> "I wanted to be with the girls. I'm not really a girlsy girl, but . . . there was just something about being able to hang out with the girls."

In exchange for breaking in leather Asolo rental boots for a local ski shop, Leslie got to use them for free.

"I remember when I finally found some boots," she said of her first tele-boot purchase. "They only brought like one or two pairs into the country that were my size—seven and half. This girl from Vermont and I were vying for them."

The skis didn't come any quicker. Leslie bought a pair of tele-skis when she was in college, but could never afford to put bindings on them. "So when I came to Breckenridge, I had skis and I was finally able to afford some bindings. The skis were 190s—the same as my alpine skis. I ended up selling them to my roommate who was a lot taller than me."

But even with ill-fitting and downright painful equipment, Leslie had been bitten by the tele-bug. "It was just so much more comfortable and it felt much more natural," she told me. "It was really exciting to be a beginner again. Just to learn something new. Just the whole challenge. It was a really exciting time."

Halfway through dinner, our conversation was interrupted by Fleetwood Mac. I again started wondering about the decisions I'd made ten years ago, about whether or not if I had stuck out my ski bum days, if I'd be a different person, a worthwhile

Leslie Ross carves by in a telemark turn in Vail, Colorado.
Photo copyright Carl Skoog, carlskoog.com.

skier. What if I had stayed in Colorado? Would I still have ended up being an underpaid journalist? Or would I still be waiting tables during the day to earn a ski pass and waiting tables at night to afford rent? What kind of sacrifice would I have needed to make to be an excellent skier?

Leslie told me she'd only recently given up her last waitressing job. To feed her ski passion, she worked many different jobs over the years—from chinking log homes, to working in ski shops, to making jewelry. She's an accomplished artist, on top of being an accomplished skier. Her own experiences as a pioneer in the women's tele-world inspired her to start Babes in the Backcountry. Not only did she want to tackle the needs of women, she just wanted some good old female companionship. After years of being ignored in the outdoor world, women's needs are finally being catered to.

"I just remember thinking, 'Where are the girls?'" she said. "During the first few years, it was fine, I was younger and I could hang out with the guys. But soon I wanted to be with the girls. I'm not really a girlsy girl, but I don't know. There was just something about being able to hang out with girls."

Her recruitment effort became Babes in the Backcountry. But more than just creating an environment where women felt comfortable learning, she wanted to present things in a user-friendly way, even complicated avalanche safety information.

"I started the Babes because I feel like the information being presented is way too techie, way too scientific," she said. "It wasn't geared toward us as recreationists. I was like, 'No wonder why no one wants to take these classes, it's way over everyone's head.' It's all data, and I didn't have a data mind. I felt like it was rough for me to get into it. And I was like, 'There's got to be a better way.'"

Leslie wanted to provide information to beginners on what types on equipment to get, what types of clothes to wear, and what magazines are out there for back-country and telemark skiers. She now even writes a regular column for *Backcountry* magazine. And as most teachers will tell you, the rewards from the students are priceless.

"The first few years I would get so exhausted preparing for the clinics. But I'd get there and the students were so energized and I was energized. It was so great just to see them so happy, and so comfortable and totally rejuvenated—like a whole new charge in life. They would come to these clinics not really knowing what they were going to get into, and they would leave and they were just—I know the word *empowered* has been overused for a long time, but that's what happened. And they gained communication skills. A lot of being in the backcountry is being able to find your voice so you can speak how you feel."

■

The waitress brought our bill. She told us we were welcome to stay around as long as we liked, and then she walked back to the kitchen. The music swelled. Giggling in the kitchen was barely audible. I thought about that blond waitress. She was probably in her early twenties, just starting her ski bum/waitressing career. Where would she be in ten years?

Leslie set some goals for herself several years ago. It was one of those things where you ask yourself where you want to be in three years, five years, ten years. She's accomplished most of what she planned for herself. Recently she had the opportunity to achieve another goal on her list. She was asked to speak at an event at the Boulder Women's Shelter. So now, in addition to teaching skiing and creating art, Leslie does something else: She's a budding inspirational speaker.

> "Before I started, I had three strikes against me. I was a female, I was a telemark skier, and I was a petite telemark skier."

"At first I was like, 'There's no way,'" she said. "I mean, what can I say that's going to inspire people? I was like, 'I don't know if I can do this.' And my friend was like, 'Of course you should do it.' And I was thinking to myself, 'This is like every part of my life. I get to this place, if I say no to this, that's basically like backing down from myself. It's not taking that challenge, not taking that risk. What is life, if I'm just going to hide?' And I realized that this was something I put out there that I wanted to do."

Leslie's talk was about mountaineering as a metaphor for life. She talked about her career as a professional telemark skier and the hurdles she had to overcome. "I talked about how before I started, I had three strikes against me," she said. "I was a female, I was a telemark skier, and I was a petite telemark skier. Those are strikes right away. When I was getting into it, there wasn't any gear out there. There wasn't any gear that fit me. And since I was a woman, no one wanted to take me seriously. I couldn't get a rep job—people were like, 'No one's gonna buy skis from a woman.' But things have changed so radically. I know some people miss how it used to be. I'm so excited about how it is now. There are so many more opportunities for women to make changes in the outdoor world, whereas before they wouldn't even be looked at."

> **"I'm so excited about how it is now. There are so many more opportunities for women to make changes in the outdoor world."**

When the music—I believe it was the Foo Fighters—became unbearably loud, Leslie and I left the Bistro. It was snowing a little heavier than before. Ski season was less than a week away. Leslie had to go home to finish final preparations for the Babes ski clinics that winter. I began the long drive back to my world in Montana.

Will I ever be able to ski like Leslie? No, but I can keep on trying.

Laura Ziemer

Passing On
the Passion

Laura Ziemer, outdoorswoman
and environmental attorney, on
Mount Barille in the Alaska
Range on the Ruth Gorge.
Photo by Jim Litch,
courtesy of Laura Ziemer.

When canoe instructor Stan Bradshaw told me that a woman named Laura Ziemer would be among my classmates in an open-water class he was teaching, I pretended to know who she was, then went home and "Googled" her. Her name calls up Web sites such as American Wildlands, Earth Justice, Tibet Environmental Watch, and Trout Unlimited. Google failed to identify her, however, as part of the rescue team involved in the 1996 tragedy on Mount Everest. I had to flip through the worn pages of my copy of *Into Thin Air*, Jon Krakauer's book chronicling the deadliest season on the world's highest mountain, to find her name. There she was, on page sixty-three, "an energetic environmental lawyer named Laura Ziemer."

Ziemer was assisting some physicians that year at a clinic in Pheriche, Nepal, "a gloomy, wind battered hamlet 14,000 feet above sea level." A foundation called

Just the Facts:
Laura Ziemer

- **Birthplace:** Indiana.

- **Current home:** Bozeman, Montana.

- **Age:** Thirty-something.

- **Occupation:** Environmental lawyer.

- **Claim to fame:** Part of the mountain rescue team involved in the 1996 Mount Everest tragedies; lawyer for Trout Unlimited; mother of Meriel, budding outdoorswoman.

- **Sports she's participated in:** Mountaineering, rock climbing, whitewater kayaking, Ultimate Frisbee.

- **Sports her three-year-old daughter has participated in:** Skiing, snorkeling, kayaking, rock climbing, flatwater canoeing.

- **Guiding philosophy as a mother:** "I wouldn't have the same quality of experience if my adventures were done by myself. It's the bond of being with other people that gives the activity such meaning."

the Himalayan Rescue Association funded the clinic, which mainly treated people suffering from high-altitude sickness and offered free treatment to Sherpas. No doubt, 1996 was a busy year for the clinic—Ziemer said there were thirteen evacuations that year.

Ziemer will talk about the Everest tragedy if you press her. She speaks eloquently and respectfully about it. You try to imagine what it must have been like, but even with her generous description, it's unimaginable. It's an event that, although in the past, creeps into her daily life.

"It's a little disarming when opposing counsel asks you, 'Are you the person in the book?'" she says. "I say, 'That's a longer story than we have time for.'"

What she does have time for these days is family. Settled down in Bozeman, Montana, with a husband and a toddler-age daughter, Laura, now thirty-nine, keeps the adventures closer to home and a little less physically demanding. She's a lawyer for Trout Unlimited and works out of a one-woman office.

With a cache of outdoor toys and a lifetime spent doing sports that some consider extreme, Laura didn't seem the type to take a flatwater canoe class. But motherhood has tamed her adventurous spirit, or at least put her in a position of wanting to introduce her passion for the outdoors to her child. Indeed, Laura wasted no time in getting her offspring outside.

Stan had told me that Laura and her husband, Shannon Prendergast, were into "death sports," by which he meant mountaineering, rock climbing, and whitewater kayaking. They'd signed up for the canoe class because they were looking for a family activity—one calm enough for three-and-a-half-year-old Meriel.

"She engaged in four outdoor sports before she learned the alphabet," Laura says about her daughter. "That seems about right.

"She's a pretty good skier. She's also snorkeled. She kayaked in the Baja when she was eight weeks old. I would hold her in a front pack and just paddle. We didn't start rock climbing until this year. She wears little boat shoes. Meriel lives to be outside. I partly credit her spending the first two months of her life outside—she got used to wind across her face, and she's pretty hardy."

■

On the day of our canoe class, Laura, Shannon, and Meriel pulled into the parking lot at a small public lake in Helena, Montana. They were a little late—they'd stopped at an outdoor store to purchase a personal flotation device for Meriel, who had a little trouble deciding which color she liked best. Spring Meadow Lake isn't particularly scenic, but it's a good place to learn, and its size and shallowness make it forgiving of most mistakes. The family's van was topped with their brand-new Mad River canoe. Meriel was fast asleep inside the vehicle—a state she remained in for most of the day.

> "I had a lot of energy and a lot of passion for becoming an environmental advocate. I think it fit in with what I was all about: climbing and going to other cultures."

Stan Bradshaw teaches canoe classes with his wife, Glenda. The Bradshaws know the relationship tester that tandem canoes can be—not that they don't get along splendidly when they're paddling together. They've been cohabiting in canoes for more than twenty years now, and teaching the finer points of paddling to others for more than thirteen.

"We don't let husbands and wives paddle together until the end of the class," Stan said. "The learning curve goes right down the toilet when they're in the boat together. It's not a negotiable rule."

Laura and I became paddling partners for the day. A lifetime spent outdoors has endowed her with the fitness of a great athlete. With her blond hair, sculpted features, and smooth-as-silk voice, she could have easily chosen a career as a spokesmodel but her ambition and intelligence led her straight to law school, with a couple of climbing detours along the way.

"I knew I was interested in environmental advocacy," Laura said. "So when I went to law school, I did a joint program in ecology and law. I was the first person to get that joint degree at the University of Michigan. I had a lot of energy and a lot of passion for becoming an environmental advocate. I think it fit in with what I was all about: climbing and going to other cultures. Environmental law was a new thing. It was a bit of a lark. It wasn't like going to law school to have a predictable, prosperous career. It was going to law school to do something people said I couldn't do—which sort of fit my personality. I was pretty unattached to following a traditional career path in law school. But in the end, it seemed to finance my passion for getting outdoors and going where I wanted to go."

> **"There was nothing more wonderful than teaching Meriel how to ski this winter. I enjoyed that more than skiing by myself."**

She's combined climbing and work in such places as Thailand, Sri Lanka, Denali, and, of course, Nepal. Sometimes the work was environmental advocacy, sometimes it was mountain rescue. While she was in Nepal in 1996, she was offered a job via fax machine with the Earth Legal Defense Fund in Bozeman. She took the job, moved to Montana, and met Shannon while playing city-league Ultimate Frisbee. Laura and Shannon married in 1998. Meriel came along two years later. It may seem unlikely for such a world-traveled adventurer to slow down and have a child, but Laura said motherhood was a conscious decision.

"It's part of the personality trait of not wanting to miss out on anything," she said. "In Sri Lanka, Thailand, Nepal—the fabric of family is so much clearer and less cluttered than it is here. Motherhood was such a profound component. Do I miss life premotherhood? Absolutely. Yet I would never trade it. There's so much more depth. It's not all about yourself. There was nothing more wonderful than teaching Meriel how to ski this winter. I enjoyed that more than skiing by myself."

Meriel, still fast asleep in the van, was unaware of what her parents were doing on the lake for her benefit. Tandem canoeing is hard enough for any two people, but when they're both accomplished outdoorspeople, it can be even tougher.

"It just seems when people are married or living together, when they get in a boat they bring in lots of other baggage from their relationship," Stan said. "It usually manifests itself when they're learning on the same level. When that happens, they implode."

"She engaged in four outdoor sports before she learned the al⟨ says about her daughter. "That seems about right.

"She's a pretty good skier. She's also snorkeled. She kayaked in the Baja when she was eight weeks old. I would hold her in a front pack and just paddle. We didn't start rock climbing until this year. She wears little boat shoes. Meriel lives to be outside. I partly credit her spending the first two months of her life outside—she got used to wind across her face, and she's pretty hardy."

■

On the day of our canoe class, Laura, Shannon, and Meriel pulled into the parking lot at a small public lake in Helena, Montana. They were a little late—they'd stopped at an outdoor store to purchase a personal flotation device for Meriel, who had a lit-

tle trouble deciding which color she liked best. Spring Meadow Lake isn't particularly scenic, but it's a good place to learn, and its size and shallowness make it forgiving of most mistakes. The family's van was topped with their brand-new Mad River canoe. Meriel was fast asleep inside the vehicle—a state she remained in for most of the day.

> **"I had a lot of energy and a lot of passion for becoming an environmental advocate. I think it fit in with what I was all about: climbing and going to other cultures."**

Stan Bradshaw teaches canoe classes with his wife, Glenda. The Bradshaws know the relationship tester that tandem canoes can be—not that they don't get along splendidly when they're paddling together. They've been cohabiting in canoes for more than twenty years now, and teaching the finer points of paddling to others for more than thirteen.

"We don't let husbands and wives paddle together until the end of the class," Stan said. "The learning curve goes right down the toilet when they're in the boat together. It's not a negotiable rule."

Laura and I became paddling partners for the day. A lifetime spent outdoors has endowed her with the fitness of a great athlete. With her blond hair, sculpted features, and smooth-as-silk voice, she could have easily chosen a career as a spokesmodel but her ambition and intelligence led her straight to law school, with a couple of climbing detours along the way.

"I knew I was interested in environmental advocacy," Laura said. "So when I went to law school, I did a joint program in ecology and law. I was the first person to get that joint degree at the University of Michigan. I had a lot of energy and a lot of passion for becoming an environmental advocate. I think it fit in with what I was all about: climbing and going to other cultures. Environmental law was a new thing. It was a bit of a lark. It wasn't like going to law school to have a predictable, prosperous career. It was going to law school to do something people said I couldn't do—which sort of fit my personality. I was pretty unattached to following a traditional career path in law school. But in the end, it seemed to finance my passion for getting outdoors and going where I wanted to go."

"There was nothing more wonderful than teaching Meriel how to ski this winter. I enjoyed that more than skiing by myself."

She's combined climbing and work in such places as Thailand, Sri Lanka, Denali, and, of course, Nepal. Sometimes the work was environmental advocacy, sometimes it was mountain rescue. While she was in Nepal in 1996, she was offered a job via fax machine with the Earth Legal Defense Fund in Bozeman. She took the job, moved to Montana, and met Shannon while playing city-league Ultimate Frisbee. Laura and Shannon married in 1998. Meriel came along two years later. It may seem unlikely for such a world-traveled adventurer to slow down and have a child, but Laura said motherhood was a conscious decision.

"It's part of the personality trait of not wanting to miss out on anything," she said. "In Sri Lanka, Thailand, Nepal—the fabric of family is so much clearer and less cluttered than it is here. Motherhood was such a profound component. Do I miss life premotherhood? Absolutely. Yet I would never trade it. There's so much more depth. It's not all about yourself. There was nothing more wonderful than teaching Meriel how to ski this winter. I enjoyed that more than skiing by myself."

Meriel, still fast asleep in the van, was unaware of what her parents were doing on the lake for her benefit. Tandem canoeing is hard enough for any two people, but when they're both accomplished outdoorspeople, it can be even tougher.

"It just seems when people are married or living together, when they get in a boat they bring in lots of other baggage from their relationship," Stan said. "It usually manifests itself when they're learning on the same level. When that happens, they implode."

After about six hours apart, Laura and Shannon boarded their canoe together for the first time. Stan described it as "entering the boat as equals." It was a literal launching into the family's future. The canoe would become their vehicle into the wilderness. Meriel stayed asleep for the maiden voyage.

■

Laura and Shannon paddled around Spring Meadow Lake as a storm slowly moved in over the mountains. Shannon took the stern seat first. The couple paddled around politely, with only a few lapses in communication. They exchanged places, Laura taking the stern. Again, they paddled around politely, with only a few lapses in communication.

A few weeks later I called Laura to see if they'd treated Meriel to her first canoe ride. They had. They'd paddled around Hyalite Reservoir, near Bozeman.

"Meriel was enthusiastic about putting her paddle in the water," Laura said. "The wonderful added bonus was that we were traveling as a family—using the boat as a vehicle for the family to move through this beautiful place, while giving Meriel a new experience. We were operating in multiple dimensions simultaneously. It was great fun for me to watch Meriel explore the whole world of a paddle and water. It was beautiful."

> "There's such a tangible connection to the sacredness of life, ironically, in a place that's so devoid of life—in the high mountains."

Canoeing on a serene Montana lake is a far cry from the violent elements of Mount Everest. Laura wouldn't trade it, though. She said that someday she'd like to travel back to the Himalaya for some trekking with her husband and daughter. But she has no desire to summit the giant peak.

The events of 1996 "made me not want to climb Everest for sure," she told me. "It . . . took me a long time to process the grief of experiencing the death of that many people in an intimate way.

"I haven't been back yet, but I would like to. The Khumbu is an enchanting place. It has a constant allure."

When Laura, Shannon, and Meriel do travel to the mountains together, Laura will be passing along her love of the outdoors, a passion that has already ignited in three-and-a-half-year-old Meriel. What does Laura hope her child gains from the shared passion?

"The answers," Laura said. "It's what's given me the greatest joy and the most profound feeling of being alive. I'm hoping she finds the same things. There's such a tangible connection to the sacredness of life, ironically, in a place that's so devoid of life—in the high mountains. Whether it's climbing or some other outdoor pursuit, I wouldn't have the same quality of experience if my adventures were done by myself. It's the bond of being with other people that gives the activity such meaning. For her, I hope it's that same sense of shared community. No matter how much or how little money she has, if she has those things she'll have a very rich life. That's been the gift of the mountains for me."

Amy Bullard

Keeping It Simple

There's no better ice climbing partner than Amy Bullard.
Photo by Peggy O'Neill.

There are a few things you might ask yourself when you're dangling from an ice ax on the face of a frozen waterfall. Not the least of which is, "What the heck was I thinking when I agreed to do this?"

The next question might be something like, "How much longer is it going to take me to get to the top of this 50-foot Popsicle?"

So you keep climbing. Swing, swing. Kick, kick. Tremble, tremble. If you can ignore your fear for a minute, you might notice that you're forgetting to breathe. After twenty minutes of pure mental stress, you find yourself at the top, where yet another question presents itself.

"What do I do now?" you yell down to the person who invited you on this preposterous adventure.

Just the Facts:
Amy Bullard

- **Birthplace:** Vermont.

- **Current home:** Bozeman, Montana.

- **Age:** Thirty-something.

- **Claim to fame:** Climbing guide for Exum Mountain Guides and Chicks with Picks.

- **Peaks she has summited:** Denali West, Mustagh Tower, Melanphulan West Face, Cho Oyu.

- **Number of minutes she has spent working indoors:** Zero.

- **Formative experiences:** Skiing on the glaciers in Austria; attending a Buddhist meditation retreat in Nepal.

- **Fun fact:** Her stone fireplace is outfitted with climbing ropes and hardware.

- **Guiding philosophy:** "Staying focused is a way to keep things less cluttered."

"Just rappel down," she says, which is easy enough when rock climbing, but when you have a sharp ax in each hand and 3-inch spikes on your toes, it suddenly becomes, well, a little freaky. It's like being a yo-yo made of razor blades.

Safely down and breathing again, you silently hope that your partner has suddenly remembered something more important she has to do and calls the whole thing off. But instead, she offers some practical advice, like keeping your heels down and relaxing your grip on the axes.

"Otherwise, you might get the screaming barfies," she says.

"Well, I wouldn't want to get the screaming barfies," you say. "By the way, what are the screaming barfies?"

She explains that it's this excruciating pain in your hands and forearms that makes you want to puke, or at least cry.

"Oh, right," you say.

You check your rope, imagining what would happen if you accidentally severed it with your ax—one of the most dangerous ice climbing mistakes. Not a nice thought, so you look up at the sky and notice the clouds are starting to clear.

You take a deep breath and start climbing again. Swing, swing. Kick, kick. Breathe, breathe. Halfway up, you ask yourself, "When was the last time I tried something new?"

The rappel down goes a little smoother, and you smile sincerely when your partner compliments you on your improvement.

During the break for lunch, you admire the beauty of the frozen waterfall, something you didn't quite notice when you were attached to it. Your pounding heart must have drowned out the pleasant sound of the water rushing below the ice surface. Varying degrees of ice thickness are defined in different shades of blue and gray.

An avalanche interrupts your thoughts when it comes crashing like a jet down a slope on the opposite side of the Pine Creek drainage. The sound is disturbing and awe inspiring at the same time. True shock and awe.

You can't help but ask, "Does anyone know where we are?" And then, "I wonder how long it would take search and rescue to find us?" But when you realize you're not in danger you think, "That was one of the coolest things I've ever seen."

Back on the ice, your picks and crampons bore more efficiently into the ice. Swing, swing. Kick, kick. Swing, swing. Kick, kick. The sound of the picks and points chipping into the ice is somehow more comforting now.

"I wonder how much ice axes cost," you think to yourself. The top of the waterfall is only a few more feet away. You slow your progress and look around at the slowly melting ice. Spring is coming to the Paradise Valley, and ice climbing opportunities will diminish soon.

You rappel for the last time that day.

"When can we do this again?" you ask your partner when you reach the ground.

■

Ice climbing is one of those things that remind you that happiness comes from simplicity. When you're hanging there contemplating your next move, you're not worrying about your neighbor who has developed a deep-seated hatred for your dog or why the hell your coworker seems to viciously ignore you when she walks by your desk. No, when you're hanging from an ice ax, 20 feet in the air, you're focused on the task at hand, which, if you're a beginner, is simple survival. This is something my ice climbing instructor, Amy Bullard, figured out a long time ago—before she had the chance to be distracted by things like prom dates, keg parties, and *Twin Peaks*. I bet if I asked her, she'd say,

> **"At sixteen I decided I never wanted to work inside. People say life is short; we all know it's long."**

"I've never heard of Twin Peaks. What mountain range is that in?"

Indeed, part of keeping her life simple is not owning a TV. Amy doesn't even think it's notable that she doesn't have one. As we're sitting on pillows in front of her woodstove and drinking tea one afternoon, I comment on the no-TV thing. She laughs as though it's odd that anyone would notice such a thing. And really it's not

Amy Bullard demonstrates safe ice climbing technique at Pine Creek Falls near Livingston, Montana. Photo by Peggy O'Neill.

that big of a deal, it's just that among the people I've met in my life, a good 99 percent of them all had TVs.

"Maybe staying focused is a way to keep things less cluttered," Amy says. I don't know if she's aware of it, but she has this habit of saying things that make you shut up and think for a minute.

"I don't have the energy to have a TV because when am I going to watch it?" she continues. "It would be another thing I would have to fit into my life and it would make me stressed out."

We quietly watch the flames flicker in the woodstove, a relaxing substitute. The smoke is sucked up a gigantic stone chimney. The chimney is the centerpiece of Amy's house, a work in progress that she and her husband, Peter Carse, work on when they're not in some faraway place climbing or leading clients for Exum Mountain Guides. The house near Bozeman, Montana, is more like a base camp for the couple, who feel just as comfortable living in a tent for three months when they guide clients in Teton National Park during the summers. But the stone fireplace is equipped with climbing ropes and hardware to make the indoors a little more tolerable.

At thirty-five, Amy can say she's never had an indoor job. She never suffered through the fast-food-stepping-stone-to-waitressing career path. Like I said, she decided at an early age to keep things simple, and she stayed focused on that goal.

"At sixteen, I decided I never wanted to work inside," she says. "People say life is short; we all know it's long. I thought being outside was so much nicer than being inside—I didn't want to waste my time. I couldn't imagine being inside, especially during the day."

Growing up on a farm in Vermont isn't a bad place to start a lifetime outdoors, even if you pick up nicknames like Supy—short for "marsupial"—or Amos just because you're a tomboy. She says she secretly spent time playing on the forbidden cliff band behind her house in addition to doing things like softball, field hockey, and running cross-country. During her second year studying anthropology at the University of Vermont, she dropped out and decided to conduct her own research on how people become the way they are. She and a friend rode their mountain bikes from Germany to Turkey and then got jobs designing a telemark ski at a German ski factory.

> **"For me, climbing has always been a meditation. It centers you. It makes you focus."**

"We'd design the ski during the week and on the weekends we got to test it out on the glaciers in Austria," she tells me. "I'd never been on glaciers before. Just having that taste of being in the mountains on glaciers, which to me represents a living mountain—the glacier moves and it's growing and it's calving off; it's ever-changing. From that point on I was hooked."

Amy did eventually return to Vermont to finish her degree in anthropology and environmental studies. She utilized the degree working a short time for Yellowstone Ecosystem Studies and the Forest Service. But she was soon off on another adventure. This time to Nepal and Thailand. At a Buddhist meditation retreat, Amy was presented with the challenge that has kept her life simple and focused.

"Halfway through the retreat, we were allowed one interview with the monk who was running it," Amy says. "I had one question. For me, climbing has always been a meditation. It centers you. It makes you focus. I feel really sharp when I'm doing it and forget about everything else that clutters my mind. So I said, 'Is it okay if I just climb instead of meditate? What would be wrong with that?' And he said, 'Nothing, as long as you use climbing to help the world. With the energy you get from climbing, like the energy from meditation, you can help make the world a better place somehow.' So it was pretty clear to me that I would end up teaching climbing. When I came home, I pursued that path of becoming a mountain guide—sharing with other people that ability to focus."

■

In the time since, she's racked up quite an impressive climbing résumé. I don't know enough about climbing to pick out the most notable expeditions. They all sound extraordinary to me: places like the Denali West buttress in Alaska, Mustagh Tower Northwest Ridge in Pakistan, and Melanphulan West Face in Nepal. There's also the all-women expedition she organized to 8,201-meter Cho Oyu in Tibet. That's the one she's proudest of. It was the first American women's expedition to climb an 8,000-meter peak without supplemental oxygen or Sherpa climbing support. After raising $54,000 by selling T-shirts, Amy and a group of six friends made the trip to Cho Oyu, whose name means "goddess of the Turquoise Mountain."

> **"It's really important for women to see that other women are doing this kind of thing. It's inspiring."**

"It was funny—the way people treated us," Amy said. "During the season, there were probably a hundred people on this mountain. It was the first time I'd climbed a mountain that other people were on. There were twelve 18-people teams. And with the hundred people at base camp, there was only one team with another woman on it. As we were going in, we'd meet these other teams and they'd say, 'Oh, are you the women-only team? Are you only women?' And I'd say, 'Are you only men?'"

Amy laughs. She's spent a lifetime in the company of men, simply because there aren't a lot of women doing what she does at the level she does it. She's not sure why that is; perhaps it's because they didn't have role models, before now.

"I think it's really important for women to see that other women are doing this kind of thing," she says. "It's inspiring. It gives us permission to do this kind of thing."

When Amy invited me to go ice climbing, I didn't hesitate. Not that it was something I had been dying to try, or that I knew she had a good reputation from teaching with an organization called Chicks with Picks. It had more to do with wanting to understand what keeps Amy so focused—how she keeps clutter from invading her thoughts. How she keeps her life so simple. After my initiation into ice climbing, I understood a little better. It's about ignoring fears and doubts and opening your mind to possibility.

Amy is making the world a better place, one climber at a time.

"It gives them a little peace of mind," Amy says. "When they're climbing and when they're learning, they're so focused. They're not thinking of all the rest of the bull in the world. Gosh, if we could have a day when everybody in the world could go climbing at the same time, it would be amazing."

We might all decide to trash our TVs.

Jody Welch

Wildlife Artist

Jody Welch, taxidermist and wildlife artist, in her Helena, Montana, shop. Photo by George Lane, courtesy of Helena *Independent Record.*

Jody Welch's handshake is like a big bear hug around your fingers. It's sincere and strong—not necessarily something you'd expect from such a petite woman. But then you notice her arms. Muscles and veins bulge under her freckled skin—not in an unfeminine way, but rather one suggesting she does things most other women don't.

Jody is a taxidermist—one of the few females in the profession in the Helena, Montana, area, and the one most likely to work on your whitetail, bear, or elk if you drop it off at Trails West Taxidermy, the shop she owns with her husband, Jeff.

Taking a break from removing the skin of a black bear, which will most likely end up on someone's floor or wall, Jody took time to do something she probably hates as much as she hates working with formaldehyde—talk about herself.

She prefers to listen to the stories of the hunters who bring in their animals. "They all have to tell you their stories," Jody explained. "That's half the fun. Some of them are great. But some are like, 'Yeah, that's a tall one.'"

Jody could tell you about her own hunting adventures with Jeff in places like Africa and Mexico, but she's got photos of her kills. The smile on her face, which brightens her whole head like a lightbulb, tells you all you need to know. If you want more details, you can look at the animals mounted on the walls of the Trails West showroom.

It's probably these photos and magnificent mounts that helped Jody develop her reputation among a group of tough-minded hunters who were initially suspicious of a female taxidermist. Even though she was the star pupil of her taxidermy class—and caught the eye of her instructor/future employer/future husband Jeff—customers were initially a little skeptical.

"The first year it was terrible," Jody said. "They'd say, 'Do you know what the hell you're doing?' If Jeff wasn't there, they wanted to make sure I measured it correctly. Most of the customers were good, but some were quite rude."

Luckily Jody's not someone who seems bothered by what other folks think. That's what led her to her profession in the first place.

Even as a child growing up in the Bitterroot Valley near Missoula, Jody was an avid hunter, when she wasn't hiking up steep canyons or picking huckleberries. She claims she was a strange child and preferred playing alone in a corner undisturbed. As the youngest in the family, she often had to find her own entertainment. "In junior high, it dawned on me—if I want to do something fun, I gotta get out there myself and not wait around for someone else. If you rely on someone else, they're going to let you down sometime or another. Some people never figure that out."

Hunting came naturally to the independent-minded tomboy. Her first gun was a Daisy BB gun. "Not a songbird was safe," she said, laughing at how PETA might take that statement.

From there she graduated to a .30-30 with open sights. "I shot one deer with it and traded it off," she said.

Her affinity for guns and hunting, however, made her a little intimidating to potential suitors. "I had a tough time finding a date," she admitted. She dumped one boyfriend after he confessed to not liking hunting: "I told him, 'You're outta here.'" Another boyfriend got the hint that his romance with Jody might be over when the saddle she'd cinched for him came loose. "That relationship didn't go much further," she said.

> **"The first year [as a taxidermist] it was terrible. They'd say, 'Do you know what the hell you're doing?' "**

When she thinks about past relationships with men who didn't quite measure up, her eyes gleam and she just shakes her head, as if saying she can't believe she went to such trouble trying to make a man fit into her lifestyle. When she talks about Jeff, on the other hand, she blushes like a schoolgirl. She says he appreciates her independence, her passion for wildlife, and of course, her artistic talent. But one of the most attractive things about him is that he knows when to leave her alone. "He came that way—already trained," she said.

Before choosing Jeff and a career in taxidermy, Jody explored some other options. She's dabbled a little in art, a hobby she'd like to spend more time on, and thinks her natural talent helps with her taxidermy mounts. She also, of course, has a keen interest in wildlife and began a college career with the intention of majoring in wildlife biology.

"I went to Montana State University for a year and majored in partying and looking for cowboys," she said. "I wanted to be a wildlife biologist, but everybody else did, too."

After the brief stint as a wildlife biology student, a few weeks in a veterinary assistant program in Oklahoma, and a short time as a dental assistant, Jody decided on taxidermy and enrolled in Jeff Welch's taxidermy school in Helena in 1989—the only female in her class. "I had already mounted ten heads on my own," she said. "They didn't look very good, but I was having fun."

After graduation, Jeff gave Jody a job in his shop and married her in 1991. Today the forty-one-year-old does most of the taxidermy work, along with Tony Ward.

Jody thinks taxidermy is a great outlet for her creativity. While many of the mounts are cast on pre-formed manikins, Jody incorporates as much imagination

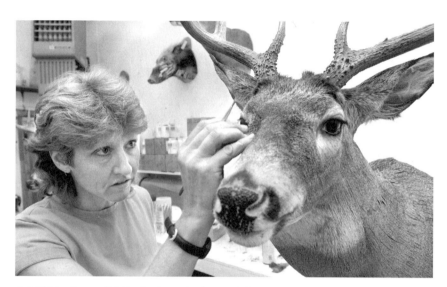

Jody Welch puts some finishing touches on her latest artistic endeavor. Photo by George Lane, courtesy of Helena *Independent Record.*

as she can. Her favorite projects are the ones she has complete artistic license with. "It's nice when guys come in and say, 'I don't know what I want,' and then you take it from there," she said.

The creativity comes in modeling the animal's expression—from relaxed to startled to aggressive. Jody finds inspiration by looking at wildlife photos in magazines and on outdoor programs on TV. But her best ideas come from what she observes in the wild. "Like art, you do best when you paint from memory," she said. "When I'm outside, I'll catch them doing stuff and I'll think, 'That would make a great pose.'"

But unlike the paintings she does in her spare time—which she usually shoves away in a closet somewhere—Jody considers her taxidermy work as "art with a deadline." Since she's dealing with a medium that can spoil if not handled properly and in a timely fashion, Jody likes to get a project finished once she starts on it. "It's not like paint—you can just add a little water to old paint and it's okay," she said.

> **"When I'm outside, I'll catch them [animals] doing stuff and I'll think, 'That would make a great pose.' "**

Jody pulled out a small oil painting that was tucked among some paperwork on Jeff's desk. It was a nice re-creation of a winter scene—sunlight reflecting off a snow-covered peak. She eyed it with criticism, looking disappointed that she hadn't done something more with it. "If it's a canvas, it's only a canvas," she concluded. "With taxidermy, you've got the whole animal—the skin, the hair—you've got more medium to work with."

> "I'm an elk opportunist. If one happens across, it's going to die, or at least get scared half to death."

Jody would like to see more women enroll in Jeff's taxidermy school. Currently the school averages about one female per year. "I don't know why a person wouldn't want this job," she said. "It's fun. It's creative. You work with your hands. You can be self-employed. And almost all my hunts are tax deductible—almost."

Her words of encouragement to other women: "Don't let the boys have all the fun."

Jody said she doesn't think being female has any special advantages or disadvantages when it comes to being a good taxidermist. "I've seen some gals that turned out some pretty ugly stuff and some that turned out some really decent stuff," she said. "If they can do a good bird and a good fish, they got talent." Jody reached into a corner of her office and pulled out a dusty fish mount. "This is the best one I did. It went downhill from there," she laughed, wiping the thing off with her shirt.

But she doesn't like to do the fish mounts anyway—too much formaldehyde involved—so she leaves the fish for her husband. Her favorite animals to work with are the same ones she likes to hunt—white-tails and black bears. She'll hunt elk, too, if she has time.

"I'm an elk opportunist," she said. "If one happens across, it's going to die, or at least get scared half to death."

It shouldn't be surprising that Jody likes to hunt alone. "I've always enjoyed my time alone," she said. "It gets your mind right." She realizes the risks, and carries a can of pepper spray if ever the need arises to scare off a more calculating predator. "Shooting someone—I just really don't want to do that," she said.

She likes the attention, though, of being a woman in a male-dominated sport. She's met a few women who like to hunt, but she said most of those women are afraid to hunt alone. And Jody's not exactly eager to become their hunting buddy. If she can't be alone, she prefers the company of men over women. "Get me in a room with a bunch of women and I'm scared shitless," she said. "It's not that way with men."

Not that Jody doesn't appreciate her feminine side. She claims to have four dresses, most of which still fit . . . she thinks. "I have to wear mascara," she said. "And I like to go to art shows. That's kinda girly, isn't it?"

"I baked two pies at Christmas," she added quickly. But something in the delivery of that detail suggested that baking was about as common an occurrence in her household as, say, a Mary Kay party.

While Jody's career and hobbies might make many women a little squeamish, Jody laughed at the thought. "Honey," she said, "I used to work in a slaughterhouse on the kill floor. I used to push around gut buggies and it never bothered me. It was actually a fun job."

Mavis Lorenz

The Company of Herself

**Mavis Lorenz with a black
bear she shot in Canada.**
Photo courtesy of Mavis Lorenz.

One of Mavis Lorenz's favorite things to say is, "You don't need a penis to pull a trigger." Admittedly, the lifelong hunter likes to shock people. Like when she tells you her age, she watches for your reaction. The fact that Mavis is seventy-six years old isn't in itself shocking, but it's what Mavis does for fun that throws some people for a loop.

Among other things, Mavis is a big-game hunter. In the last few years, she's gone bear hunting on Vancouver Island, sheep hunting in the Northwest Territories, and caribou hunting in Alaska. The hunting trips were in addition to her other travels, including a bike trip down the length of the former Yugoslavia, a two-month car-camping trip in Europe, a hitchhiking trip in New Zealand, and a recent trip to Pakistan and Inner and Outer Mongolia.

Just the Facts:
Mavis Lorenz

- **Birthplace:** Wisconsin.

- **Current home:** Missoula, Montana.

- **Age:** Seventy-something.

- **Claim to fame:** Passionate big- and small-game hunter.

- **Occupations:** Root beer stand waitress; movie theater usher; assistant lifeguard; professor of physical education at the University of Montana.

- **Closest brush with failure:** She once got a D in a college psychology class.

- **Contents of garage:** Discarded bike tires, skis for all occasions, empty microbrew bottles, trophy buck antlers.

- **Guiding philosophy:** "I really don't give a damn what other people think."

Most people who meet Mavis make comments like, "I hope I have her energy when I'm that old." Being less than half her age, I know I won't have her energy when I'm that old. I don't have it now, and I never did.

On a cool October morning the weekend before the opening of rifle season, I met Mavis at her home in Missoula, Montana. She had reserved that day in her busy schedule to go hiking in the Sapphire Range, just south of Missoula. I, unwittingly, invited myself to go along with her.

"Bring your mountain bike, too," she had told me.

■

Forever and favorably unmarried, Mavis lives like a college student. Given her former profession as a physical education professor at the University of Montana, this shouldn't be too surprising. But most single, childless, seventy-six-year-old women I know don't have garages full of discarded bike tires, various types of skis for different snow conditions, empty microbrew bottles, and trophy-size antlers waiting to be mounted. Even her vehicle, a four-wheel-drive pickup truck, looks like it belongs in the driveway of a fraternity house rather than in front of the home of a senior citizen who delivers meals-on-wheels to folks her own age. The pickup is full of discarded paper cups, miscellaneous plastic eating utensils, extra layers of clothing, and several old pairs of glasses, which, as she informs me, were all from the dollar store since her only requirement is magnification.

I shove my bike next to hers in the camper mounted on her pickup and we start the drive to the Sapphires. Mavis has three objectives for the day: looking for elk sign, figuring out where a particular road intersects with another road, and, hopefully, shooting a grouse if one happens to cross our path. To achieve these objectives, Mavis has brought along a twenty-pound fanny pack of essential tools including maps, emergency fire starter, a pistol, and a dog collar equipped with a radio transceiver—her neighbor knows what frequency to check in case Mavis ever fails to make it home. More times than not, Mavis is alone when she's hunting.

How does a woman become so comfortably independent in the backcountry and so well prepared for anything, including death, in places that challenge the strongest men?

Mavis doesn't know; she's just always been that way. And she's always preferred the company of herself. Growing up in a rural town in Wisconsin in the 1930s, Mavis was ten years younger than her closest sibling.

"What a surprise I was," Mavis says and laughs. "What a blessing."

■

She might have been the apple of her father's eye had he not been working so hard as an electrician and handyman to keep his family afloat during the Great Depression.

"We were poor as church mice," Mavis says. "My dad got paid in everything but money. We got paid a whole hog or a half of beef or a backyard full of firewood. One time we got a piano. Being the lowest man on the totem pole, I had to take piano lessons. This woman had hired him to do some painting. Instead of paying him, she gave me piano lessons. I hated it. I lasted maybe three weeks. It was awful."

Mavis preferred playing outside with the boys; it was the beginning of her lifelong love affair with the outdoors. She also developed an affinity for hunting squirrels and pheasants, something other girls weren't doing.

"There were more boys in our neighborhood than girls, and the girls were kind of boring," she says. "And so I was always playing games and did outdoors kinds of stuff with the boys until I was about twelve. When they realized I was a girl, they didn't want to have anything to do with me anymore."

When her sisters failed to finish college, Mavis's father figured Mavis was in for the same future. He refused to pay for college tuition.

"I thought, 'All right, you son of a gun. If you're not going to give me any money, I'm going to do it on my own.' Which I did," she says.

Many of Mavis's stories follow the same plotline: challenge presented, challenge

Mavis Lorenz outfitted for a day's hunting. Photo courtesy of Mavis Lorenz.

taken, and successful conclusion. In fact, when asked if she'd ever failed at anything, the best she can come up with is a D she got in a college psychology class. She also mentions her failure to get married, but that was her own choice.

"When I was thirty, I was dating somebody, and I said, 'Oh geez. Should I or shouldn't I?' When I turned forty, I said, 'I think I made the right decision. It's too late now.' When I turned fifty, I knew I made the right decision. When I turned sixty, no problem. When I turned seventy, well, here I am."

As Mavis put it, it was a great escape.

"I was really quite selfish," she says. "I wanted to do things and go places, and I knew I couldn't do that if I got married. In our generation, if you got married, you had children. I didn't want to be tied down. That's why I say I'm selfish."

■

After an hour's drive up a spiderweb of logging roads, Mavis pulls her truck over and parks it with the engine pointed downhill—in case there are battery problems, she says. We drag our mountain bikes out, and she explains the strategy. We're going to follow the road, which was recently designated nonmotorized, and find the highest point possible to leave a bike parked so it can be used to haul out the carcass of any game she might shoot. Mavis's bike is equipped with racks and panniers for such a venture. She also has a gun rack mounted to her handlebars, on which she can carry a rifle or shotgun. But today is just for scouting, so the only gun she carries is the pistol in her fanny pack.

We alternate riding and pushing our bikes while watching for elk tracks in the dirt road. I have it easy. Being ill prepared for disaster, I have only my twenty-six-pound bike and a light fanny pack that holds a water bottle, my sandwich, and a notebook. I've failed to bring even a bike-tool kit or an extra tube in case of a flat tire. Mavis, on the other hand, has the twenty-pound-fanny-pack-with-everything-you'd-need-if-you-were-stranded-on-a-desert-island strapped to her already heavy bike. After about an hour, I offer to trade bikes. I push the thing maybe about 400 yards and am grateful when Mavis suggests we ditch the bikes and just hike for a while.

We sit down for a spell and a funny thing happens. A four-wheeler ATV comes buzzing by. The driver, dressed in full camouflage, stops to chat. As I said before, Mavis likes to shock people. Sometimes she says something that knocks you over like a charging elephant; other times she does it so subtly that you don't know you've been taught a lesson until a few days or years later.

"Let's be nice to him," Mavis says before the law-breaking ATVer shuts off his engine.

The thirty-something driver is charmed to find an old woman out on a hike this lovely October afternoon. He even acts amazed to see a mountain bike next to her. But when Mavis starts entertaining him with stories of the forty years she's hunted in these mountains, he acts a little nervous, though still friendly. And when she breaks the news to him that he's breaking the law on his motorized vehicle, he accepts it as if it's the first time he's heard it. I don't know if he's realized, to this day, the irony

> **"The salary was pitiful. It still is. But the hunting and the fishing and the mountains and the hiking and the backpacking and the river system and the whole schmear was a good fit. I've never been sorry."**

of a seventy-six-year-old female hunter scouting for elk on foot and mountain bike while he drives his young—albeit a little overweight—self around on an ATV.

■

Mavis is to physical fitness as Anna Nicole Smith is to sloth. She lives it, she breathes it, and she made a career out of it. Inspired by her grade school PE teacher, young Mavis set a course to follow in her role model's footsteps. After earning enough money working at a root beer stand, as a movie theater usher, as an assistant life-guard, and in various capacities in farmers' fields, Mavis went to La Crosse State College (now the University of Wisconsin at La Crosse). It was the same college that her favorite teacher had attended. When Mavis graduated, she took a job at the same school where her mentor had taken her first job. Mavis then decided she wanted to teach at the col-lege level, so she accepted a teaching assist-antship at the University of Washington, where she earned a master's degree. When the University of Montana offered her a job in its PE Department in 1954, Mavis thought it was the perfect match.

> **"Well, I'm jogging along on the highway, going to St. Ignatius, when I meet a highway patrol-man. . . . He said, 'Something wrong, lady?' 'No,' I said, 'I'm just getting some exercise.' 'Huh?' he said."**

"The salary was pitiful," she says. "It still is. But the hunting and the fishing and the mountains and the hiking and the back-packing and the river system and the whole schmear was a good fit. I've never been sorry."

Mavis claims that she was jogging before jogging ever became cool. She would jog to her jobs at the root beer stand, the theater, and the swimming pool, which was almost a mile loop.

"I remember one time I went back to visit friends and relatives back there [in Wisconsin] and I jogged," she says. "I was going downtown. And I overheard some old farts who were just sitting there in front of the barbershop saying, 'There goes that Lorenz girl. She's still running and she hasn't caught anyone yet.'

"And another time I came back from a teachers' convention when I was living here in Missoula and came back on a Saturday," Mavis continues. "My friends were already parked in front of my apartment. I ran in the house, threw down my suitcase, grabbed my pack and my skis, and jumped in their car for a weekend of skiing up at Whitefish. After having sat I don't how many hours, both in riding to and riding from the convention and sitting in meetings, I was rump-sprung. When we got up to the bison range, the bison were pretty close to the road so my friends wanted to

A Tribute to Women Who Hunt with a Man

She follows behind him not knowing his plan.

Her rifle on shoulder with carrying sling

She follows his heels, sees not a thing.

When footsore and weary, she asks for a break

He tells her let's wait till we get to the lake.

So hours later, without seeing a track

He announces intentions of circling back.

As the daylight is fading fast into dusk

He calls off the hunt that turned into a bust.

Instead of traipsing around after him,

Pick a good spot, perhaps on a rim.

Build a little fire to keep yourself warm.

You can sit there for hours without any harm.

When he finally returns without any luck,

You can proudly show him your three-by-four buck.

You field-dressed it out knowing that job, too!

You were taught by the women BOW crew.

—Mavis Lorenz
Becoming an Outdoors-Woman (BOW) instructor

stop and look at them. I said, 'Okay, I'm going to jog down the road and get some exercise. You can pick me up on the way.' Well, I'm jogging along on the highway, going toward St. Ignatius, when I meet a highway patrolman. The first thing he did was turn around and pull alongside me. Then he said, 'Something wrong, lady?' 'No,' I said, 'I'm just getting some exercise.' 'Huh?' he said."

■

Mavis and I walk up an old jeep trail for a while then stop and eat lunch. I've known lots of hunters in my life, even some of them women. But the women hunters I know hunt because their husbands hunt. To me, Mavis is something different. She's developed the passion on her own.

"It's getting out in the woods, getting out in the outdoors," she says. "I really enjoy the wildlife and the birds and the flowers, the whole scene. It's a challenge. You are trying to find an animal that can hear—I don't know how many times— better than you can. That can see much, much better than you can. They know their territory. You're in their backyard. So they have all the advantages. The only advantage you have is a high-caliber rifle. The challenge is in trying to get close enough to them to see them. And so many times you don't see anything. But it's like when I was in Dillon [Montana] last week. In the first afternoon of hiking I saw eleven deer. The second day I saw seven more deer, a golden eagle, a rough-legged hawk, and a moose. So you can say I didn't get anything . . ."

She gets the memories, she gets the thrill of being outdoors, and she gets the stories. Sometimes she gets to share the stories with someone else.

"We had a bowl of soup and hot chocolate with bourbon in it and the northern lights and my trophy sheep was there. What an experience!"

Mavis sold her motorcycle to calm her sheep fever. She shot a sheep in Montana and wanted to shoot another species. Sheep permits don't come easy or cheap. The funds from the motorcycle went toward a $16,000 sheep hunt in the Northwest Territories of Canada. After hunting several days, Mavis made a clean shot through the heart of a Dall sheep at almost 400 yards.

"That guide hit me so hard over the back, and said, 'Mavis, that was one damned good shot.' When we got back to base camp and I told the gang what he'd said, they were astounded. They had never even heard him curse. We had gotten back to camp at three in the morning. The northern lights were in full glory. Ohhhh." Mavis sighs. "We had a bowl of soup and hot chocolate with bourbon in it and the northern lights and my trophy sheep was there. What an experience! It was great. That's what I love about hunting."

■

On the walk back to our bikes, a blue grouse scurries along the road in front of us. Mavis pulls the pistol out of her pack and hands the pack to me. "Here, hold this," she says, "and stay behind me."

Mavis sneaks quietly up the road, stops, and aims at the unsuspecting bird. With a steady hand, she shoots but misses, and the bird scurries up a hill into some brush. She climbs after it and spots it again within firing range. Again, she takes careful aim and fires. The fat grouse takes to the air and flies off. We hear it crashing through branches several hundred yards downhill from us.

"Damn. There goes tomorrow night's supper," Mavis says.

Mavis straps the pack onto her bike, and we begin the rocky descent back to her truck. She tells me to ride behind her in case the pack falls off. I want to blame the weight of her bike for the fact that she descends so much faster than me. But I know it's something else—fearlessness.

"Yeah, people tell me that," she says. "I'm pretty confident in my abilities to do things, but I'm pretty conservative. If I get to a point where I'm uncomfortable, I back off. I'm comfortable in my own position, in my own person. Maybe that's my ego talking again. But I really don't give a damn what other people think. I don't want to be doing things, marching to a different drumbeat, to be a show-off. I want to do it for my own satisfaction. It's a challenge. You don't need a penis to be brave to do this stuff," she says and looks at me to gauge my reaction.

Pam Houston

Pretending to Be Pam Houston

Pam Houston, author and river guide, paddles away.
Photo by Kae Penner-Howell, courtesy of Pam Houston.

During those years between college and graduate school, those years that some of us remember fondly as the "slacker" years, I read a book. Well, I read many books, but one in particular got me off the path to professional underachievement. I was living at my parents' house in Austin, Texas, slacker capital of the world, and planning a strategy to return to the Rocky Mountains, where after being handed a BA in English I immediately moved to a ski town to pursue a career in waitressing. If I had been a better waitress, I might still be in Steamboat Springs skiing and serving bread bowls filled with bad chili. But as luck would have it, I sucked at waitressing. When it came to serving food to obnoxious vacationers, I realized I'd rather do anything else, even if it was move back to Texas to live with my parents and ponder law school.

Just the Facts:
Pam Houston

- **Birthplace:** Pennsylvania.

- **Current home:** Davis, California, and southwestern Colorado.

- **Age:** Forty-something.

- **Claim to fame:** Outdoor and adventure writer, author, and director of the creative writing program at the University of California, Davis; licensed river guide.

- **Books under her belt:** *Cowboys Are My Weakness* (short stories); *Waltzing the Cat* (short stories); *A Little More About Me* (essays). She is finishing a novel.

- **Pam on writing:** "There are moments of joy, but not a lot of them."

- **Guiding philosophy:** "My reason to be here is to have whatever experience I have and transform it onto paper."

So anyway, back to that providential book. It might sound more intellectual to tell you that it was, say, Kate Chopin's *The Awakening* that changed my life. But, no, it was a little book called *Cowboys Are My Weakness* by Pam Houston that got me thinking and dreaming. It's a collection of short stories revolving around women's relationships with men. Specifically, women's relationships with outdoorsy-type men, and those women trying to be equally impressive outdoors. Even more precisely, it was a book about my life thus far, so I thought. It was one of those moments when you think something like, "If this person can write something like this and have it published, then I can do it, too." It's moments like those when you easily forget that things like talent and resources are also necessary.

When you identify someone as your role model, you do what you can to follow in her footsteps. When you fail at that, you grasp at the thinnest of similarities between you and the person whom you can only plead to St. Anthony that you might someday be mentioned in the same sentence with, uttered by someone other than your mother. I enrolled in a graduate creative writing program at the University of Colorado because I knew Pam had done a graduate creative writing program at the University of Utah. Indeed, her master's thesis was *Cowboys Are My Weakness*. UC Boulder also fit in nicely with my yearning to return to the Rocky Mountains.

I remember the first day of my ultimately useless career as a creative writing graduate student. There was a reception at some nicely preserved historical building on campus for all the English graduate students. It was exactly the kind of party that you would imagine a bunch of literary-minded, dressed-in-black, theory-touting grad students would throw—a pretentious ballyhoo. To distinguish myself from the pompous, I pronounced my admiration of Pam Houston, which was as well received as a blister on the first day of a weeklong backpacking trip. I don't think anyone meant to disparage my personal hero, but I was among a group of writers who aspired to be Hemingways, Faulkners, and Steins.

I suffered through two years of writing workshops, pretending to be Pam Houston on weekdays and escaping to the outdoors on weekends. I can't say those were particularly productive years—I became a little distracted by the man I eventually married. But I did keep track of Pam's career as an outdoor and travel writer. She wrote another book of fiction called *Waltzing the Cat* and also several essays and articles, which appeared in magazines such as *Ski, Outside, Travel & Leisure, Elle*, and *Vogue*, and which were eventually collected and published in a book called *A Little More About Me*.

Several years after my graduate school days, I find myself as an outdoor writer for a small paper in Montana wondering how I ever got into this racket. Sure, you can't beat writing about skiing in the winter, biking and hiking in the summer, and fishing in the spring and fall. But I can't do this forever. As I write this, I look down at a bruise on my right calf the size and precise dimensions of a particular rock I grapple with every time I ride my mountain bike on the trail behind my house. I usually get the best of that rock, but last week it grabbed hold of my front tire and wouldn't let go until I took a spill over the handlebars. My left wrist, shoulder, and chin are scabbed from another tumble I care not to discuss since it is the result of a maneuver I should be smart enough and old enough not to attempt. It could be Pam's fault. She led me down the path, after all.

Just by chance, I happened to read the *Washington Post* online one Sunday, when the *Washington Post Magazine* featured some sort of summer-reading series. I was reading a lot of stuff online those days since I was laid up with a sprained ankle. One of the stories was by Pam Houston. It wasn't an outdoorsy piece. Rather, it was a story about her childhood and a woman named Martha Washington—a babysitter of sorts. In it Pam tested the close relationship with her hero Martha, by letting a friend come between them and forcing Pam to act in a way that wasn't in her nature. It was a lovely story and it got me thinking about my old hero.

■

It's surprising how easy it is to track down people these days. Through a series of

Internet searches, I found Pam's e-mail address and begged and flattered my way into a phone interview with her. I'd never spoken to her before in my life. In fact, the only exchange I've ever had with a famous person was when I served Ned Beatty a tuna sandwich in Steamboat Springs.

Pam Houston is a busy person. Most days she's the director of the creative writing program at the University of California, Davis. When she's not doing that, she's teaching writing workshops in places like Aspen, Ouray, Taos, and her ranch in southwestern Colorado. She must take time in there somewhere to do a little writing, as she has a novel coming out soon. We had arranged an interview during the rare extra time when she had nothing else to do, or rather no other human being to talk to—while she made a grocery run from her ranch to Denver—a four-hour drive with no other companions but her dogs, a collection of Irish wolfhounds and mutts, and her cell phone.

> "The landscape opened up my imagination. . . . The mountains and canyons gave me permission to write."

It's not every day that you get to talk to your personal hero. What can you ask without sounding stupid? How can you make yourself sound more interesting than you actually are? Why did I get myself into this? There are no good answers to these questions. You just kind of wing it and hope for the best. That's all you can do.

I sat in the ugliest room in our new old house—the yet-to-be-remodeled computer room with pink carpet and Little Bo Peep wallpaper. Pam sat at the steering wheel of her car, with a clear view of some of the most scenic driving in the United States. Luckily, I could picture the scene through her windshield—I had driven those same roads many times during my years in Colorado—the years I spent pretending to be Pam.

I asked her about her childhood and other biographical information—stuff that is easy to ask about when you're nervous, stuff that I knew the answers to from reading her stories and essays. I won't pretend to be Pam here and rehash all that in my own clumsy words; you can read about it in her eloquent prose.

What's important to know about her past that makes her evolution as a writer and as a human being relevant is that an abusive childhood while growing up in Pennsylvania and New Jersey caused her to have a hard time trusting people and a hard time letting people into her life, she says. But now at age forty-one, having just celebrated a first wedding anniversary with her second husband, Martin Buchanan, she's drifting away from what got her career off the ground—writing about landscape and somewhat superficial relationships with men—and into true human drama.

The conversation we had that morning was selfish on my part. I was probably seeking answers for my own future rather than thinking of questions that would make a good story. But here's what transpired.

∎

P. O.: At what point did you realize you could combine your passions for writing and the outdoors?

P. H.: I guess when I came out west when I finished college. I rode my bike across the country. When I graduated, I wanted to do something. We did the Maritime Provinces of Canada. We camped out, got in shape, and managed not to get killed. Then since I was in shape, I decided to ride out west. But I ran out of money in Grand Lake, Colorado. It wasn't my first time seeing the Rockies—I had been there a few times with my parents. But this time, it was like, "Wow this is where I'm supposed to be."

The landscape opened up my imagination. It seemed very natural. When I was first interviewed, I thought of my outdoor life and my writing life as complementary. I think less so now. The mountains and the canyons gave me permission to write. That was the drama I could write about. I wasn't good at writing about human drama. I saw my own personal landscape in the outdoors. There's nothing like wilderness for healing: You don't have to trust anyone, and you don't. You are by yourself. It's quiet. It was critical. I've done that healing. Now I'm more interested in people. When I look out the window, the stories it unlocks for me are more about a community than being in the wilderness.

> **"There's nothing like the wilderness for healing. . . . You are by yourself. It's quiet. It was critical."**

P. O.: What is the writing process like for you? Do you write every day?

P. H.: Not even close to every day. I write in kind of spurts. I don't have a very regimented work ethic. I go for weeks, sometimes months without writing—real writing—fiction. Then all of a sudden I'll write twelve, fourteen, sixteen hours a day. It's my process. I take big breaks and let things percolate.

> **"If you have experiences that are very precious to you, whether it's awful or wonderful, the actual writing of it gives it away, it changes your relation- ship to it."**

Fiction is what I'm more vested in. It's the hardest and most rewarding. Creative nonfic- tion is a viable form. Fiction is the thing that I sweat blood over. Personal essays come quite easy to me.

You know, because I write from my per- sonal life, I don't make a huge distinction on whether or not it really happened to me. My rea- son to be here is to have whatever experience I have and transform it onto paper. I seem to be different from most writers that way. Once something happens to me, it seems obvious to commit it, to trans- form it to a story or essay. To me, it's not that much more difficult to write about a miscarriage than to write about a spa in Hawaii. It's finding the signif- icant details to tell a story in my life. This is what I do—I have experiences, then when they are ripe, I write them down.

If you have experiences that are very precious to you, whether it's awful or wonderful, the actual writing of it gives it away, it changes your relationship to it.

P. O.: Do you feel like you are helping to make the world a better place?

P. H.: I've been told that I have. I get letters from people. People whom I meet in person tell me that, too, and it means a great deal to me.

I love to teach because at times when I think writing is the strangest, most self-obsessed, fashiony profession, teaching reminds me I'm doing something good. In teaching, I'm helping others tell their story. With writing, I go back and forth with that. I think, "Yeah these stories help people. They're entertaining. They make them feel not so alone."

But sometimes I think I may as well be making culottes.

With writing I go back and forth about its values, but with teaching I never do.

P. O.: Do you enjoy writing when you're in the actual process?

P. H.: I'm never sure of the answer to that question. After years of saying no, I've discovered that what I don't enjoy are the five minutes before writing. Getting ready to write is the awful, awful part, and the avoiding writing, which I do a lot of. Once I have my butt in the chair, once I'm actually doing it, there's a part I enjoy. I'm just now realizing that. I used to think that the only reason you wrote is because it was more awful when you didn't. *Enjoyment* is the wrong word. In the writing, there are moments of joy, but not a lot of them.

P. O.: Is there something you'd rather be good at?

P. H.: There are things I am good at. I'm a good cook—I can't bake to save my life, but I think I could have been a pretty good chef. I'm really good at organizing trips. I would have made a good wilderness travel planner.

One thing I really want to be—my mother was a stage actress, Martin is an actor—I want to be a playwright. That is a goal of mine.

Then there are times—writing is so sort of vague—that I wish I was a landscaper or just could mow lawns. I have a longing to do something where you see the progress—mowing the lawn you see that square that needs to be mowed get smaller and smaller.

P. O.: Tell me about Martin.

P. H.: He's a stage actor. He's thirty-four. I'm a total worrier. He's just the opposite. He's calm and he's sweet. He's a nerdy guy who loves show tunes. He's not particularly ambitious. He works, he acts. He doesn't really care where. We met and he proposed within a month. I could see it coming—I could see it coming. "Okay," I thought, "there's a lot of ways to say maybe." Then he got to the end of the long-winded, overdramatic proposal, and I said yes. It's really sort of mysterious to me. It's looking like one of the smarter things I ever did.

I'm more like the guy and he's the woman. He takes care of the house and the animals. On the wedding day I had the typical male freak-out. He hired someone to come over to give me a pedicure. He said, "Maybe you should commit to the pedicure." After the pedicure, I felt great. Then we got married.

P. O.: Do you think you got where you are by a series of accidents and coincidences or did you have a definite plan?

P. H.: I did not have a life plan that I was aware of, although I think I did as it turns out. I never could have articulated it other than to say, "I wanted to be a writer." Which is a small way of describing my life. But I have a growing faith, faith in writing, faith in metaphor. Faith is a medium to tell my stories and to understand myself. But also to have faith that everything is put in our paths and we need to recognize it. My difficult childhood made me a very keen observer. As a result, I'm good at saying, "Aha! There's something I should grab a hold of."

Appendix:
Resources for Women's Outdoor Adventures

Lori-Ann Murphy
Reel Women Fly Fishing Adventures and Guide School
P.O. Box 289
Victor, ID 83455
(208) 787–2657
(208) 787–2691 (fax)
www.reel-women.com
info@reel-women.com

Susan Eckert
AdventureWomen, Inc.
15033 Kelly Canyon Road
Bozeman, MT 59715
(800) 804–8686 (in the U.S. and Montana)
(406) 587–3883 (outside the U.S.)
(406) 587–9449 (fax)
www.adventurewomen.com

Alison Dunlap
Alison Dunlap Adventure Camps
Western Spirit Cycling
478 Mill Creek Drive
Moab, UT 84532
(800) 845–2453
alisondunlap.com

Lena Conlan
Crossing Latitudes
(800) 572–8747 (U.S.)
(406) 585–5356 (phone and fax)
(46) 70–670–1153 (Sweden)
www.crossinglatitudes.com/index.htm
info@crossinglatitudes.com

Leslie Ross
Babes in the Backcountry
Empower, LLC
P.O. Box 8227

158 Bucyrus Circle
Breckenridge, CO 80424
(970) 453–4060
www.babesinthebackcountry.com
leslie@babesinthebackcountry.com

Amy Bullard
Chicks with Picks
www.chickswithpicks.net
(970) 626–4424

Mavis Lorenz
Becoming an Outdoors-Woman
(program available in forty states)
Montana Fish Wildlife and Parks
P.O. Box 200701
Helena, MT 59620-0701
(406) 444–2615 (Liz Lodman)
www.fwp.state.mt.us/education/outdoorswoman.asp
llodman@state.mt.us

Other Interesting Web Sites
www.lunachix.org
www.nwtf.org/wito (National Wild Turkey Federation's Women
in the Outdoors)

Peggy O'Neill

Author Peggy O'Neill
on the Missouri River with
a rainbow trout.
Photo courtesy of Peggy O'Neill.

About the Author

Peggy O'Neill lives in Helena, Montana, with her husband and son and a black Lab named Bruce. This is her first book, and unless she is fired from her current position as the outdoor editor of the *Independent Record* newspaper, probably her last. In her spare time she skis, hikes, mountain bikes, backpacks, fly fishes, and does whatever else she can to avoid writing.